What Kind of Life Do You Have in Mind?

It is the most open secret of all the ages—you create your own reality. The state of your life began in, and is maintained by, the images and beliefs in your own mind. What you receive from the world is just what you expect from it. What you give to—or withhold from—the world is the result of who you believe you are.

Therefore, the key to changing your life for the better lies in the ability to change your thoughts and beliefs. Easier said than done? Yes, if you don't know where to begin or how to let go of your negative programming.

Mind Magic was written to let you accomplish the miracle of transforming your life by transforming yourself. Marta Hiatt, an experienced psychotherapist, gives you a full set of easily mastered techniques including self-hypnosis, guided visualizations, and self-healing affirmations. These tools will let you erase the negative mental patterns that poison your life and let your light shine as it was meant to.

Dr. Hiatt also explains in clear, non-tecnical language why these methods are so effective—and reveals some surprising truths about the role of consciousness in the universe.

About the Author

Marta Hiatt, Ph.D., holds a doctoral degree in Counseling Psychology and is a California State Licensed Marriage and Family Therapist. Dr. Hiatt held seminars in the San Francisco Bay area for twenty years, teaching people to become more creative and successful in their personal and professional lives.

To Write to the Author

If you wish to contact the author or would like more information about this book, please write to the author in care of Llewellyn Worldwide and we will forward your request. Both the author and publisher appreciate hearing from you and learning of your enjoyment of this book and how it has helped you. Llewellyn Worldwide cannot guarantee that every letter written to the author can be answered, but all will be forwarded. Please write to:

Marta Hiatt, Ph.D.
% Llewellyn Worldwide
2143 Wooddale Drive, Dept. 978-1-56718-339-9
Woodbury, MN 55125-2989, U.S.A.
Please enclose a self-addressed stamped envelope for reply,
or $1.00 to cover costs. If outside U.S.A., enclose
international postal reply coupon.

Many of Llewellyn's authors have websites with additional information and resources. For more information, please visit our website at www.llewellyn.com.

Marta Hiatt, Ph.D.

MIND MAGIC

Techniques for Transforming Your Life

"The simple secret of the universe is you create your own reality!"

Capt. Edgar D. Mitchell, Apollo 14 astronaut

Llewellyn Publications
Woodbury, Minnesota

Mind Magic: Techniques for Transforming Your Life © 2001 by Marta Hiatt, Ph.D. All rights reserved. No part of this book may be used or reproduced in any manner whatsoever, including Internet usage, without written permission from Llewellyn Publications except in the case of brief quotations embodied in critical articles and reviews.

First Edition
Seventh Printing, 2008

Book design and editing: Michael Maupin
Cover design: Gavin Duffy
Interior illustrations: Tom Gatica

Library of Congress Cataloging-in-Publication Data
Hiatt, Marta.
    Mind magic : techniques for transforming your life / Marta Hiatt.
    — 1st. ed.
       p.   cm.
    Includes bibliographical references and index.
    ISBN 13: 978-1-56718-339-9
    ISBN 10: 1-56718-339-5
    1. Self-actualization (Psychology) 2. Consciousness. 3. Self-perception.
    4. Health. I. Title.

BF637.S4 H52 2001
158.1—dc21   2001023439

Llewellyn Worldwide does not participate in, endorse, or have any authority or responsibility concerning private business transactions between our authors and the public.
    All mail addressed to the author is forwarded but the publisher cannot, unless specifically instructed by the author, give out an address or phone number.
    Any Internet references contained in this work are current at publication time, but the publisher cannot guarantee that a specific location will continue to be maintained. Please refer to the publisher's website for links to authors' websites and other sources.

Llewellyn Publications
A Division of Llewellyn Worldwide, Ltd.
2143 Wooddale Drive, Dept. 978-1-56718-339-9
Woodbury, MN 55125-2989, U.S.A.
www.llewellyn.com

Llewellyn is a registered trademark of Llewellyn Worldwide, Ltd.

Printed in the United States of America

Acknowledgments

My great appreciation to my editor, Dot James, for her invaluable contributions, loving support, and many hours of hard work, improving and elucidating this book. I am also thankful for all the assistance and most helpful suggestions provided by Michael Maupin, my editor at Llewellyn Publications. Many thanks to Tom Gatica for his creative artwork in designing the diagrams that enhance this book.

I am also grateful to all of my students, from whom I have learned much over the years, and my psychotherapy clients who, through observing them struggling with and resolving their problems, have taught me a great deal about the wondrous workings of the human mind, and how to live a successful life in this "best of all possible worlds."

To those great souls, both here and hereafter,
who have most inspired me,
Edward L. Crump,
Catherine Higdow,
and Dr. Thurman Fleet
of the Concept-Therapy Institute,
this book is lovingly dedicated.

Contents

List of Illustrations

The greatest discovery of this generation is that human beings can alter their lives by altering their attitude of mind.

ALBERT SCHWEITZER

Introduction

As a psychotherapist working in private practice, I see people every day who have created havoc in their lives through misuse of their emotions. I have seen the same people turn their lives around dramatically through contacting the tremendous power within them and using it constructively.

The greatest power in the world is inside your own head. It's called the subconscious mind. The ability to correctly program this incredible force within you can transform your personality and create miracles in your life. Knowledge of the dynamics of your subconscious mind can bring you excellent health, financial prosperity, self-confidence, peace of mind, loving relationships, and whatever else you desire in your life. It can also help you overcome the negative concepts that create anxiety, depression, poverty, poor health, and lack of friends or lovers. In the realm of the subconscious, there is a *vital force* that can help and guide your life, if you will only listen to it, learn its laws, and program it correctly. Used incorrectly or ignorantly, that same fantastic power can produce an existence of living hell. It all depends on your ability to deprogram it from the negative concepts that others have given you, and reprogram it to positive ones. *If you want to know what you've been asking for, just take a look at what you've got!*

We all determine the direction of our lives, but most of us do it unconsciously, and the consequence is often chaos. To a very great extent, we create our own reality, and we are responsible for what we attract into our lives through our own thinking. Through using your mind constructively, you can unlock dormant potentials within you, alter inappropriate behavior patterns, overcome the negative conditioning from your past, and increase your creativity and self-confidence.

Richard, a biochemist I counseled some years ago, was a good example of how we can use the power of our subconscious mind to create a better life. Richard came to see me because of personal problems that were overwhelming him; he was particularly concerned because he had been searching for a job for over a month and had been unable to find one. He was highly qualified, with a master's degree in chemistry, but his despondent attitude was preventing him from finding the position he so desperately wanted. He grew up in a poor family and had worked two jobs to put himself through college, but his parents had "poverty consciousness," and were convinced that even a degree wouldn't do much good. Richard subconsciously bought this negative idea.

I taught him how to make "money affirmations," a technique I learned from Leonard Orr, instructor of "Prosperity consciousness" seminars in San Francisco. Because Richard was an intellectual and a scientist, he thought I was a little crazy to suggest that writing affirmations would get him the type of job he wanted, and at a higher salary. Reluctantly, he carried out my suggestions and was amazed to find they worked. Within three weeks he found a job at an excellent salary with an expense account and a company car.

Another client, Nancy, a fifty-three-year-old divorced woman, had attempted for three years to find a man with whom she could spend her remaining years. After two disappointments in marriage, one lasting twenty-five years and the second only a year and a half, she felt she was too old to attract the type of man she desired. Three years of making the rounds in the "singles scene" had left her already shaky self-esteem even more severely damaged, and she came to see me in a state of severe depression. After a few months of working with methods to increase her confidence and self-esteem, I taught Nancy how to use the power of her subconscious mind to attract a suitable companion. She diligently applied these principles for several months, then started getting telephone calls from men she had met in the past, and met new ones through friends who began inviting her to social affairs. Within a year I received a letter from her; she had moved to New York with her new husband and was extremely happy, having at last found the fulfillment for which she had long been searching.

When I was twenty-one years old, I enrolled in a course called Concept-Therapy. I was living in Toronto, Canada, at the time, and was a shy, self-conscious, constantly ill young woman with no belief in my own abilities. I managed to complete the course, but it took me three years to find the courage to enroll in the concomitant study group meetings. The first time I went to a meeting, there were only five other people present. Even so, when the textbook was passed around so that each of us could read a paragraph from it aloud, I was too shy to do so and had to hand the book to the next person.

Learning more and more about the power of the mind, I decided to try imaging myself being more confident. I sat down every day, morning and evening, for about ten minutes, and concentrated all my energy on seeing myself standing before a group, relaxed, perfectly poised, and speaking clearly and confidently. The first step was to get the feeling over to my body that I really had the confidence I desired, which was very difficult because I had never experienced it. If I were a confident woman, I decided, I would probably hold my head up high, pull my shoulders back, and look other people directly in the eye. I walked around my apartment *acting as if* I had great self-confidence.

A month after I began my imaging the leader of the study group asked me if I would introduce the speaker at the next meeting, a gathering attended by some thirty people. Since I had made a pact with myself that I would never turn down an invitation to speak, I nervously accepted, feeling my heart skip a beat as I said "okay." A month later, after visualizing every day, I did it! I was nervous, true, but I didn't fall to pieces; and I didn't lose my voice or faint, or suffer any of the other disasters I had previously anticipated. Delighted with my initial success, I continued visualizing myself as self-confident. Eight years later, when I moved from Canada to California, I had conquered my inferiority complex to such an extent that I have now presented lectures before hundreds of people.

More and more people today are learning, as I so fortunately did early in my life, the methods for harnessing the tremendous power of the subconscious mind. Astronaut Captain Edgar Mitchell declared, "The simple secret of the universe is: you create your own reality!"

Your understanding of the profound significance of Captain Mitchell's wise words can change your life dramatically. My objective is to share with you a variety of techniques you can learn to use your potential to the fullest, and become as successful, happy, and prosperous as you want to be. Every one of us has mental powers and abilities that are lying dormant. We can awaken these by applying proven methods for getting in touch with the Great Power within us. These techniques are not new; they have been well documented by New Age researchers, as well as in the lives of successful men and women who have learned the secret of tapping the inner power of the subconscious mind. You can join their ranks; all that is required is that you learn and apply the techniques for transformation that follow.

Although many books have been written on a single technique for improving one's life, this book presents a variety of proven methods, while at the same time explaining *why* and *how* these life-transforming techniques work.

The book is divided into two parts. Part One is a study of the nature of consciousness, and how our minds work. To use the techniques for transformation most effectively, one must first understand the nature of the mysterious "something" we call *consciousness*, which permeates all life. This section explains in clear, nontechnical language why the power of the mind is so effective in producing change in one's life. Rather than ask you to rely on faith alone in using these methods, data is presented from psychology, philosophy, and parapsychology to demonstrate how the mind functions, and how consciousness expresses itself in mankind as the life force behind all thought and action.

Part Two is a practical handbook on how to apply the theory explained in Part One, and includes guided visualizations, self-healing techniques, affirmations to attract love and prosperity, and methods of inducing self-hypnosis.

If the reader is not interested in the philosophical discussion presented in Part One, he or she may skip this section and begin using the techniques given in Part Two.

The Evolution of Consciousness

Consciousness must be a part of nature or, more generally, of reality, which means that, quite apart from the laws of physics and chemistry as laid down in quantum theory, we must also consider laws of quite a different kind.

NEILS BOHR, *Physics and Beyond*

Today there is a wide measure of agreement, which, on the physical side of science approaches almost to unanimity, that the stream of knowledge is heading towards a non-mechanical reality. The universe is beginning to look more like a great thought than like a great machine.

WERNER HEISENBURG, *Physics and Beyond*

ONE
Attributes of Consciousness

To use the techniques for transformation most effectively, it is helpful to understand the nature of consciousness. To fully comprehend who we are as beings in the world, we must attempt to understand this mysterious "something" we call consciousness, which animates all life forms. Because the story begins way back in our biological history, we will explore how it has expressed itself from its first manifestation in the world of matter, on up to the fully developed human being.

Let's begin with a brief look at the atomic and subatomic phase of creation, because this is as far back as we can go to ascertain what this creative power, manifesting in all of life, has been doing in its long evolution. To understand our own nature, we must go back to our ancient beginnings and examine the orderly process of creation. We'll consult authorities that have dealt extensively with the subject: theology and science, including evolutionary biology, psychology, and philosophy, since these disciplines have given us all the information we have about ourselves as beings in the universe.

What Is Consciousness?

No one really knows what consciousness is, but we do know its main attribute, which is *the ability to receive and respond to impressions from outside stimuli.* Therefore consciousness, in the cosmic meaning, is a state of recognition or responsiveness, no matter how minimal, and this ability exists even within a tiny electron.

Within the atom, consciousness manifests itself in a very basic form of attraction and repulsion. When two electrons (negative particles) are brought into proximity, they try to avoid each other; there appears to be a factor of recognition, a kind of "conscious knowledge" on a very fundamental level. Yet there is neither a brain nor a nervous system to register these impressions; it happens without any physical mechanism whatsoever. This suggests that electrons possess an attribute of consciousness, a type of *receptivity* in a very elementary form. Like particles repel each other, and a field is set up whereby they try to move out of each other's way. How do they recognize another particle as being either positive or negative without any sensory equipment to record these impressions? We postulate that the electrons have "consciousness" on a minimal level.

If consciousness is in every atom, and atoms are present in every cell, it therefore follows that consciousness is present throughout our human bodies. This is what we mean by saying we are alive: this consciousness is flowing through us and sustaining us. *Consciousness is the one and only reality in the universe,* manifesting itself through different forms. Thus we can conclude that there is consciousness within all forms of matter, from submicroscopic particles of energy, on up to humankind.

The universe either began with these subatomic particles floating around in outer space, or they were always present. Nobody knows. But we do know that, gradually, over eons of time, they began to group together and, as a result, the physical universe eventually came into being. It is only logical to assume that this didn't suddenly happen one fine day because of a giant cosmological accident, as some scientists have speculated, but that this Creative Power within the electronic particles must have had some plan of operation in the construction of the universe, because we see incredible order and harmony—a symmetry and pattern that no accident could produce. We deduce from this that the material universe is the result of an *image* projected by this Creative Power, whatever it may be. An image that has become visible, therefore, is one manifestation of consciousness. A later chapter will discuss how to use this attribute to effect changes in your life through mental visualization, a technique for transformation.

Our hypothesis, then, is that there is a Creative Force, which we call consciousness, which evolved the natural universe out of itself, and which is the vital energy maintaining and sustaining everything in existence. Given this premise, let us briefly examine the nature of this force as it manifests itself in the universe, so that we can discover some of its other attributes. To do this we will progressively examine the evolution of consciousness as depicted in the following chart (Figure 1, page 6).

Consciousness in the Atomic Realm

Science states that, in the beginning, *if* there was a beginning, only electronic or subatomic particles existed. Science neither admits nor denies the existence of God, but merely states that, since God cannot be analyzed, tested, or measured with physical instruments, the subject is not a fit study for scientific analysis.

Thus, science ignores the question of the Creative Power by giving us the theory of subatomic particles as the starting point of all creation, and declares that it cannot go beyond that.

If we turn to theology for answers about the beginning of creation, we are told that everything proceeded from the First Cause, God. Theology teaches that there was a definite, historical beginning to the universe, that God exists, and that this Being created the world. They claim this theory requires no proof because the evidence resides in the simple fact that the universe is here and, since our minds cannot conceive of something created out of nothing, God must therefore have created it. Certainly, all of our experience on earth indicates that every effect has its antecedent cause. Therefore, it seems logical that something must have set this cosmological process in motion, and something must be maintaining it. The question of *what* that something is however, is quite another matter.

In mentally constructing the beginning of the universe, science speculates there was once nothing but infinite space, although "nothingness" is a difficult concept for our minds to

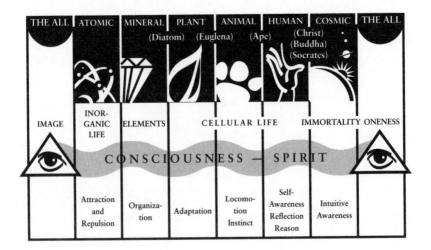

Figure 1.   The Evolution of Consciousness.

grasp. Ultimately, this space became filled with countless electronic particles that eventually grouped together into atoms, and then into molecules of matter. The question then is "what Great Intelligence started this process eons ago which eventually formed the universe, and what sustains it in its function?" At our present state of knowledge, we can give only one answer: consciousness. This is the starting point for everything.

Consciousness in the Mineral Realm

The great American political writer Thomas Paine wrote, "The only evidence you will ever get of the Creative Power is from studying nature." That is where we begin in order to understand this consciousness inherent in all life forms. If we start by examining the mineral phase, the lower end of the evolutionary continuum, we discover another attribute of consciousness: each mineral is crystallized according to a definite design or image. For example, untold billions of snowflakes fall upon the earth each winter; they all have six points, yet no two of them have ever been found to be alike. Whatever this power is, it certainly doesn't lack creativity!

There are many different kinds of crystals, but the pattern for the particular shape that each one will take is embedded within its atomic structure. The pattern of a quartz crystal, for instance, is a basic idea, an *image* in nature that can be repeated again and again. Just as the pattern, or image, of the oak tree is within the tiny acorn, so too is the image of the human being contained within the microscopic DNA strands of the fertilized egg in the mother's womb. When you were so tiny that it would have required an electronic microscope to find you, the blueprint, or image, for the color of your eyes, the thickness of your hair, the structure of your bones, and all your other physical characteristics, was already established. As we will try to show, the Divine Plan for our lives is also incorporated into that blueprint, for us to discover through introspection and meditation.

The question naturally arises: where did the basic pattern for a quartz crystal, or an oak tree, or a human being, originate? To any thinking person it is clear that some kind of intelligent force (consciousness) must have started with an image, which ultimately manifested itself as a particular form.

The first principle of all creation is that everything begins with a plan, or image. If you were to build a house, you would naturally begin with a plan in the form of a blueprint. It is the same with building a life, but very few people are aware of the necessity of having a definite plan for their lives. Consequently, they flounder about and don't know where they're going, or why. Today we often read scary stories in the newspapers asserting that the baby boom generation is not saving enough money for retirement, and may have to continue working after age sixty-five. For those to whom this projection will become reality, the cause is usually lack of a plan. It makes no difference what you want to accomplish; you must start with a clear image of your objective and, the more perfect your idea, the more perfect will be your creation. Conversely, the sloppier your idea, the sloppier the result.

Consciousness in the Plant Realm

Advancing along the evolutionary continuum to the next stage of creation, vegetation, we discover that plants, too, have a minimal level of consciousness. One way this is demonstrated is by photosynthesis. This process, whereby plants manufacture their own food by using sunlight, indicates that there is a vital intelligence within the organism.

Consciousness is the fundamental reality throughout all life, but it manifests itself in varying degrees, with different attributes. The consciousness of a rose is no different in kind from that which manifests itself as an electrical current flowing through a light switch; the consciousness in inanimate, inorganic matter, or in a human being, is only different in degree from that in the electrical current. Consciousness is the one and only reality, alike in kind, but expressing itself in many degrees. Research documented in Brett Bolton's *The Secret Power of Plants* shows that plants have a kind of cellular consciousness, and can somehow tune in to all forms of life. In his book, Bolton tells the story of Cleve Backster, a polygraph expert in New York, and former specialist with the CIA, who published an article in the *International Journal of Parapsychology* titled "Evidence of a Primary Perception in Plant Life." Using a polygraph (lie detector) he found plants register apprehension, fear, pleasure, and relief. They respond to overt threats to their well-being and have definite and sympathetic responses to other living things. Backster's findings seem to indicate that plants have feelings and some sort of telepathic communication system with other forms of life. In one experiment Backster hooked up his houseplants to his polygraph machine when he went out of town, then took careful note of his activities. Comparing his notes to the graph, he found his plants' greatest emotional response came when he decided to return home. They also registered what in humans would be considered agitation when he was almost hit by a car. In experiments designed to see if plants react to threats to their well-being, he decided to burn a leaf with a match. At the instant he thought of lighting a match, there was a dramatic change in the polygraph tracing. The pen activity had gone wild and almost shot off the chart! Other experiments have shown that plants grow stronger and more luxuriant when exposed to classical music, compared to hard rock.

In the plant phase of creation, we see *cellular life* for the first time, a vastly significant advance in consciousness. One of the chief characteristics that plants exhibit, which is not found in inorganic material such as rocks, is the ability to adapt. For instance, a tiny fern will push its way up through concrete or pavement if it must. I'm always amazed to find weeds growing in the tiny cracks of my walkway. One day I went to get some potatoes I had stored in my basement, and found they had somehow discerned the direction of a sliver of light from the small window, and turned their sprouts toward it. A tiny sapling will adapt to the fierce blowing of the wind in a storm by bending its branches, otherwise they would be snapped off. A cutting from certain plants, such as a geranium, if planted, will adapt to its new situation and develop specialized root cells where there were none before. This is a high degree of adaptation, and this principle applies to humans as well as plants.

The greater the ability to adapt, the higher the consciousness within a form. The organism that survives is always the one that has the ability to adapt itself to its environment. Darwin's principle of "the survival of the fittest" didn't mean the largest or strongest; if it did we'd still have dinosaurs walking the earth. The organism that survives is the one that has the greatest ability to adapt. To our dismay, we all know that cockroaches fall into this category, and they've been here for millions of years.

Human beings have adapted amazingly well to the natural world, conquering cold, rain, and heat, blasting through mountains to build homes, colonizing deserts, forests, and seashore, digging oil and gas from the earth, and harnessing nuclear energy. Unfortunately, many humans have not developed the attribute of adaptability in their personal lives; they resist their circumstances and become unyielding toward life. Neurotic people, for example, characteristically develop a rigid way of reacting to every situation. They cannot deviate from their inflexible behavior patterns no matter the circumstances, so they are defeated by their inability to adapt and devise more effective ways of responding to life. A secretary I know came to work one morning to find her IBM Selectric typewriter replaced by a computer. A tutorial was installed in it that would teach her how to run the various software. She glanced at the accompanying book and froze at her desk. No way was she going to learn how to run a computer when her typewriter had been perfectly adequate all these years. Because of her resistance to adapt, she subsequently lost her job.

Some time ago a neighbor of mine was promoted to vice-president, but then realized he was too anxious to give speeches before the other executives at meetings, so he quit. These neurotic patterns underscore an inability to adapt to changing circumstances, which can result in illness. In his book *Who Gets Sick: Thinking and Health,* Dr. Blair Justice states: "Disease or dysfunction is the body's way of saying that we have failed to adapt, adjust, or change to meet the situation, and we have done so at the price of physical or mental disturbance."

The attribute of *adaptability* is characteristic of the mature, psychologically healthy person. In fact, we could say that rigidity equals pathology, and fluidity equals health, in both the physical and mental realms. In this tense, stress-filled world, those who survive without breaking down are people who are capable of making the necessary adjustments to the changes wrought by increasingly sophisticated technology. If a person rigidly and continually resists change, he or she will be broken by life, just as a resisting tree can be broken by a powerful wind. There are some people who make a career of fighting the politicians, the establishment, the anti-environmentalists, the pro-environmentalists, the status quo, or any change to the status quo, and on and on. While activists are needed in every society to help keep the people in power honest, those who dedicate their lives to constantly fighting change instead of adapting to some of it will lead unsatisfying lives.

Though consciousness expresses itself in various forms, there is really no fixed dividing line between the different phases of creation: it's just a gradual blending as this consciousness begins expressing itself through higher and more complex models. An example of this gradual transition is the euglena, a green aquatic plant that manufactures its own food through photosynthesis, as plants normally do. When the euglena is in darkness, however, the green coloration temporarily disappears. It propels itself by moving its little tail, called a flagellum, through the water, feeding on bacteria. Locomotion and digestion of animal matter are characteristics of the next highest phase of creation, the animal realm, so we might say that the euglena is a "missing link" between the plant and animal kingdoms.

Consciousness in the Animal Realm

As every animal lover knows, animals can perform some truly remarkable feats, even though they lack the fully developed reasoning ability of a human. Consciousness expresses itself in this phase of the evolutionary continuum primarily through instinct. Instinct in the animal realm is a wonderful guide. It leads the wild duck to sense the coming winter, and to fly thousands of miles south from its northern home to a pond in a warmer climate—the exact same pond its ancestors landed on the year before, and the year before that, ad infinitum.

It is instinct that tells little Muffin it's 5:30 P.M. and you should be pulling into the driveway at any moment. Although she can't tell time, she's got her own internal clock, and she runs to the front door when you're a couple of blocks away. She also knows that you won't be home in the afternoon when she puts a paw up to the refrigerator door, opens it, and pulls down some food. But she instinctively puts a slinking, guilty look on her face that lets you know immediately she's been bad.

A bee cannot fly, according to the science of aerodynamics, because its body is too bulky for its delicate wings. Fortunately the bee doesn't know this, so it buzzes from flower to flower, guided entirely by instinct. Even more remarkable is the ability of certain crustaceans and echinoderms, such as the lobster and starfish, guided by instinct, to grow a new limb if one is lost.

While instinct is a perfect guide for an animal, it cannot be improved upon, so an animal is locked into what it already knows; it must keep performing the same actions in the same way, just as all its forebears have done for centuries. But humans are not doomed to such repetitious behavior. In addition to instinct, we possess the highest quality that consciousness manifests, *self-awareness.*

Consciousness in the Human Realm

Self-awareness, or reflective thought, is the main attribute distinguishing humans from animals. It is the consciousness that enables us to think inwardly and to contemplate ourselves. Reflection is the power to turn one's consciousness upon oneself, to know oneself and, especially, to *know that one knows.* Humans are the only creation in the universe who can be the object of their own reflection and, because of that, another world is born: an inner world, a reality in which no lower animal can ever participate. Incapable of contemplating itself, or of being aware of itself as the conscious subject, not even a higher type of animal such as a dog or cat, that knows who its master is and where its food is, can know that it knows. In consequence, it is denied access to a whole domain of reality in which mankind can move freely. Systems of physics, philosophy, mathematics, and astronomy, for example, have all been constructed because of man's unique ability to reflect inwardly. Because of this new attribute, *self-awareness,* we have a host of expanded abilities: abstract reasoning, free will, creativity, foresight in order to plan ahead, and many others.

It is indeed a great treasure to be aware of oneself. Since this is the characteristically human quality, the more aware one is, the more fully developed he or she is as a human being. Our culture, however, is oriented toward reducing one's self-awareness, rather than expanding it. We often have the television on in the morning while we're preparing to go to work, so we turn our consciousness outward; we listen to talk radio as we drive to the office, or perhaps listen to our own voice talking on our cell phone, then we are preoccupied with work for eight hours. When we arrive home we often absorb ourselves in the television once again, or reading the paper. In all of this we have almost no time for self-reflection, for contemplation, or connecting with our inner self. Although we alone have this great gift—self-conciousness—we don't use it fully. In fact, we often suppress it and instead act robotically, walking around in a semi-trance. All of the great mystics and spiritual leaders have admonished us that we are asleep, and our great task in life is to wake up and become fully conscious.

Advanced consciousness, therefore, is measured by self-awareness, the ability to think inwardly, to reflect upon oneself, to contemplate one's inner nature. If this is the indication of a higher consciousness, it follows that *the greater the ability for self-reflection and self-awareness, the more advanced the consciousness,* or the more evolved the soul. A highly developed person, such as Socrates, Thomas Merton, or Maya Angelou, for example, would spend a great deal of time contemplating inwardly to get in touch with his or her inner self. If we examine the lives of all great thinkers, we will discover that they set aside some time each day for inner reflection, which is the most direct path to higher consciousness. If you wish to know who you really are, you must stop long enough to reflect upon yourself. The importance of such contemplation and meditation will be discussed in chapter 8.

Since the animal has only *simple* consciousness and does not have *self*-awareness, its consciousness is always directed outwardly toward finding food, mating, avoiding enemies, etc. However, even in the least evolved human being, for example, the primitive bushman, there is at least a faint degree of the inward direction of consciousness, or reflective thought. Humans can intellectualize, conceptualize, and analyze experiences and compare them with previous ones. Homo sapiens, the most marvelous life form in the universe and the apex of creation, have evolved from the animal plane of simple consciousness to self-consciousness. There is but one reality, and that is consciousness. It is all-inclusive, but expresses itself in varying degrees.

The highest expression of it on earth is for us to be able to say: "I am."

In this vast evolutionary process we can see consciousness expanding itself through the perfecting of exquisitely complex and efficient nervous systems and, especially, in the formation and development of the human brain. Our highly perfected brain is the center of consciousness, and consciousness is the heart of evolution; it is the Creative Force itself, for each human being is "consciousness in expression." Consciousness is the one and only reality in the universe, and it manifests itself through different forms.

There are three levels or types of consciousness, as represented by the following diagram (see Figure 2). This is the structure of the universe: various *degrees* of development, or consciousness, high, low, and in-between. A newborn human baby begins life on the border between animal and human consciousness. It has the potential for self-consciousness and reflective thought, but these qualities are not yet developed. At a certain stage in the child's maturation, at approximately two years of age, it begins to

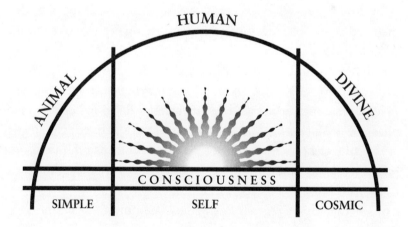

Figure 2.   Degrees of Consciousness.

become aware of itself as a separate entity, and the sense of separateness is born. The child is becoming humanized and developing *self*-consciousness.

Humans are suspended between the animal and divine phases of evolution, but we have the capacity to attain greater heights of consciousness. The highest achievement of humanity is the triumph of rationality: the ability to reason and act logically, to create science, philosophy, and technology, and to plan for the future. The problem with human evolution is that we have not yet learned how to use our newly developed gift, rational thought, wisely. We have not learned how to reason properly, and how to handle our emotions constructively. In psychology, philosophy, and theology—the three systems which should be able to teach us how to live—there is enormous confusion, contradiction, and contention. Each person is put on earth to accomplish something, which is to evolve consciousness to higher levels while on this planet, so that the Creative Power may have greater expression through each individual form. Some people are developing toward their highest expression but, unfortunately, many others are actually regressing and becoming more animalistic than any beast.

In developing self-awareness, we have not achieved the ultimate goal, for our destiny as human beings is to continue to evolve toward *cosmic consciousness*. Just as humanity progressed from biological evolution through neural and cultural evolution, we now need to engage in a process of evolving our individual consciousness. Remember that a division between one phase of evolution and another is not rigidly defined. The chart is just a model to demonstrate that there is a continuum of consciousness, and that this whole complement is latent within each of us, as part of our biological heritage. Throughout the ages we can see that this Creative Power has been molding matter and consciousness so that both may become more perfect expressions of spiritual consciousness. It is constantly in a state of "becoming," evolving itself into higher and higher expressions as it manifests itself through form. That which is in evolution cannot be an absolute; it cannot be a fixed "thing," such as a god who has the attributes of a glorified man.

The animal realm is guided solely by instinct, and therefore it cannot interfere with the perfect operation of the Creative Power. Because of this, the undomesticated animal is free from all of the various diseases that plague mankind. In the animal realm there are only some dozen or so diseases to which animals in the wild are subject. In the human realm, there are over three thousand different disease categories. What is the major difference between the human and animal worlds? The ability to reason abstractly. Obviously, something has been wrong with the way we have used our reasoning ability because the human world is filled with strife, violence, and mental and physical illnesses.

It was only when self-awareness began to develop, with its singular power of originating ideas, that many of the various forms of disease appeared. Other than congenital disorders and infections caused by outside sources, autoimmune and organic diseases such as arthritis, coronary problems, and cancer, always have an emotional and lifestyle component. The intimate connection between mind and body makes us vulnerable to a variety of diseases. Every thought we have produces an immediate physiological response, although it may be minimal. Over time, negative thoughts such as anger, fear, and sadness have an impact on the body, which can eventually result in disease. We have all heard of "Type A" personalities, personified in the hard-driving, aggressive, combative executive who drops dead of a heart attack at fifty. The stress a lion experiences while chasing its evening meal is very different from that a person has to deal with when the boss is calling him on the carpet, and there is a direct relationship between our emotions and our health. The executive's "self-awareness" gives him the ability to internalize the boss's criticism and make judgments about himself, which creates stress. In contrast, the lion cannot reflect on his actions.

Because we have the power of choice, human consciousness is the only form that can work against the inherent plan within it. The power of choice implies a tremendous responsibility, and some of us obviously have been choosing irresponsibly, judging by the state of the world. If you make choices that interfere with, or are contrary to, the Creative Power within you, that interference will always manifest itself internally in your body, or externally in your life.

Each one of us is a part of the all-pervasive consciousness of the universe, and our ultimate evolution is beyond the powers of the imagination! This consciousness is the power that is sustaining you, and it can be contacted and directed when you understand its laws. This, then, is our great task in life, and that is what life is all about: to keep evolving our consciousness until we attain unity with the Creative Power within us. In order to achieve this it is necessary to learn how to think properly, and how to channel our emotions into constructive ends. We have the freedom to go against our own purpose for being, our own innate plan, our inner image. We can interfere with it and cause chaos, and that inner disharmony is always manifested, either in the body through physical illness, in the mind through neurotic or psychotic symptoms, or externally in confusion and unhappiness in our lives. We must learn how to make the right choices for our lives in harmony with the great cosmological plan. In order to do that we need to understand how consciousness, the great Creative Power of the Universe, operates within human personality, how our minds become programmed to ideas, and how to change these ideas if they are destructive. We will explore these areas in the following chapters.

Everyone who is seriously involved in the
pursuit of science becomes convinced that a
Spirit is manifest in the Laws of the Universe—
a Spirit vastly superior to that of man, and one
in the face of which we, with our modest
powers, must feel humble.

ALBERT EINSTEIN

TWO
The Great Power
Within You

Having explored the attrib-
utes of consciousness in the previous chapter, let's look
at how consciousness expresses itself in human personality. Our spiritual, or higher, self has been called
by many names. The New Testament gospels speak of
it as "the Kingdom of Heaven within a man," "the
mustard seed," "the pearl of great price." Muslims
call it "the secret," and say it is closer to man than
breathing. In Chinese wisdom it is "the Jewel," "the
Diamond Center," "the Pearl that the dragons guard."
Plotinus called it "the Soul-Center," others have called
it "the Oversoul." The chiropractor names it "the
Innate Mind," the psychologist, "the Unconscious."
But, say the Taoists, "the name that can be named is
not the eternal name."

Anything that we can say about the Creative Power is therefore symbolic, and all verbal descriptions of it must necessarily be inaccurate and incomplete. Even those who have contacted this reality through a transcendent, mystical experience have not the words to describe it because it is beyond the realm of thought and language. The ultimate reality can never be discerned by our rational, reasoning mind, thus insight into it will be a nonintellectual experience that will arise, if we are so fortunate, in a nonordinary state of consciousness. In the Eastern traditions, it is a perceptiveness that lies outside the realm of the intellect, obtained by a mystical experience, by "mindfulness" rather than thinking, and by taking the time to look inside oneself.

The Upanishads say about it:

> There the eye goes not,
> Speech goes not, nor the mind.
> We know not, we understand not
> How one would teach it.

Spirit Within: The Creative Power

In attempting to understand the cosmos, we usually put science in one corner and theology in another, but their differences are not as extreme as we have assumed; there is an integration between some of the basic tenets of both approaches. To demonstrate this ideological synthesis, we will use both the theological and psychological terms for understanding human personality. Theoretically, psychology has divided the mind into two parts, the conscious and subconscious (or unconscious). To show the correlation between the psychological and theological teachings, we will use these terms, but we will also use the religious term, soul, for the conscious part of the mind, and Spirit for the subconscious. The term Spirit represents that Unknowable Power that first manifested itself in electronic particles, and is now manifesting in us. This name is synonymous with consciousness. Although Spirit is all-pervasive in the universe, in human personality it seems to have its central focus within the subconscious realm. Without our conscious awareness, it takes care of all our bodily functions, such as beating our heart and circulating our blood.

At the moment of conception, a single cell of life was created from the joining of sperm and ovum, and we were just a tiny speck of matter smaller than the head of a pin. The question then is: when those two cells united to form a microscopic cell, was that *you?* Were *you* there? If a human being consists of body, mind, and soul, as most of us have been taught through traditional religion, none of these could have been present at your conception. There was certainly no body developed, and there could be no mind because the mind is dependent upon the brain, and the brain was not yet formed. As to the existence of the soul at conception, we must turn to the scriptural definition. "God breathed into man's nostrils the breath of life; and man became a living soul" (Genesis 2:7). Since there were no nostrils at conception, and no "breathing," if we accept this statement literally, the soul had not yet developed.

If you were not there, then what was there? Logical reasoning offers only one answer: the Great Unknowable Power, which we call Spirit, must have been there. *Some* type of consciousness had to be present in that single microscopic cell to develop into a fetus, create all the organs, the tremendously intricate brain and spinal cord, and all the other incredible complexities of your fully formed body. Spirit was within you at the moment of conception, and then it divided that one cell into two, and then divided each resulting cell again and again until, in the short space of approximately 280 days, you emerged comprised of some 63 trillion cells. And every one of those cells, from first to last, contains Spirit, just as every cell of your adult body still contains the Creative Power of the universe. Consider for a moment the great wonder of this!

There is another unfathomable mystery. The DNA strands that contain the blueprint of the "baby-to-be" are within the nucleus of each cell, and they replicate themselves when a cell divides. Even though each cell duplicates itself exactly, soon certain cells begin to specialize, becoming heart cells or hair cells or skin cells. How do they do this? How do they know what they are supposed to become since they are all alike? No one knows, but it is obvious they must be directed by an *intelligent consciousness,* which we call Spirit.

Because Spirit is in all of our cells, its job is to keep our bodies functioning normally. The conscious mind cannot perform internal physiological tasks because it doesn't know how. If you consciously had to beat your heart for the next five minutes, for example, you would die because you would not know how to get blood up to your brain.

Consider, for example, that you could not walk if you had to do it with your conscious, reasoning mind; you don't know what muscles to use, and in what sequence, and with what amount of exertion, in order to keep from falling on your face. A little thought will show that we would not live through the night if our conscious mind had to keep beating our heart, drawing air through our lungs, and circulating our blood, so there must be another power in charge of this aspect. Or, consider a mother who gives her milk to her baby. What happens next? The mother doesn't know how to turn milk into blood and bones and lymph, and everything else her baby needs in order to grow, and neither does the baby. We can recognize from this that we are dealing with a Conscious Entity within us; there is consciousness experiencing all of life, and it is experiencing a little part of it through that baby, and through you. Think of it—the Creative Power of the universe is not up in the sky somewhere, but resides within your own being!

Spirit will take care of our bodies perfectly as long as we don't interfere with it. If our heart or liver or digestive system isn't functioning properly (unless there is a genetic disorder), somehow we have interrupted the orderly direction of the Power Within through incorrect thinking, improper care of the body, or misuse of our emotions. If you have inadvertently created some disease within your body, you can correct it, for the *power that made your body can heal your body.* You will learn how to do this in chapter 9 on self-healing, because this Power within us can be contacted and directed if we understand its laws.

Spirit is all-pervasive in the universe; there is something beyond our little ego-self, and the effect of discovering it will transform and elevate and recreate the life of the one who knows it. Using this knowledge is the means by which a person becomes their true self. When you understand that, you usually begin to serve as an instrument for this power to help uplift the consciousness of the world. When the realization fully dawns upon a person that Spirit, the Creative Power of the Universe, resides within their own being, they become sublimely able to handle any problems and transform their life and relationships, because this Power is an active, dynamic force that can be consciously directed, and it will do whatever we ask of it.

In his wonderful book *Memories, Dreams and Reflections,* the great psychologist Carl Jung wrote: "The decisive question for man is: Is he related to something infinite or not? That is the telling question of his life. Only if we know that the thing which truly matters is the Infinite can we avoid fixing our interest upon futilities, and upon all kinds of goals which are not of real importance. If we understand and feel that right here in this life we already have a link with the Infinite, then our desires and attitudes change." Jung was a discerning man who recognized that human anxiety is directly traceable to a longing to be reunited with the Divine Source of one's being. That is what everyone is looking for through various means, although it may be called by different names.

Occasionally, I'm asked, "Do you believe in God?" What the questioner is really asking is: "Do you believe in *my concept* of God?" No one can believe in anyone else's God. The only God you will ever know is the one you come to personally identify with, the one that you discover through an individual, inner experience within the silence of your own heart. That is the only God that can ever exist for you, and it can never be discovered by the intellect alone. Infinity, the supreme degree of consciousness, is beyond the comprehension of our rational mind, although many people have purported to describe it. We can call this Power God, or Jehovah, Allah, Nature, Infinite Mind, Almighty Being, the All, or a host of other appellations; but what is important to realize is that Spirit is *within us*. It's not a domineering, authoritarian, capricious, wrathful entity, as God is so often depicted by unenlightened clerics, but rather it is an active, beneficent, and creative Power.

We hypothesize that there are four aspects to human personality: body, mind, soul, and Spirit. This theory departs from traditional religion that teaches there are only three aspects—body, mind, and soul—and places Spirit (or God) outside human personality, residing somewhere in the heavens. This is the great error in those teachings, for the Creative Intelligence is within us, just as it is within everything else in the universe. God is not locked up in some church building, and one does not have to be in a specific place to revere creation. God is not formal; you don't have to wear a jacket and a hat in order to commune with the Divine Presence, which is ever-present. God is not solemn and does not have to be approached with a long face and a bowed head. Most importantly, God is not invisible. If we merely open our minds and eyes, we will see that all of life is but a manifestation of this *One Consciousness*, through different forms. As Walt Whitman wrote: "Every moment of the light and dark is a miracle, every cubic inch of space is a miracle."

Whenever we are moved by the higher aspect of our being, such as when we are listening to a beautiful piece of music, feeling love toward someone, or watching an exquisite sunset, we are in contact with our higher self. This is what all our yearnings really are, the longing to reunite with Spirit. "Our hearts are restless," said St. Augustine, "till they rest in Thee."

The Ego and Self-Identity: What is the Soul?

For centuries much controversy has raged about the meaning of the term soul, primarily around the question: "Do I have a soul, or am I a soul?" Genesis 2:7 states: "the Lord God breathed into man's nostrils the breath of life, and man *became* a living soul." According to this passage, the soul must be something that one *is*, not something that one *possesses*. Yet many followers of traditional religion think of the soul as a possession they are in danger of losing, a nebulous, ghost-like entity that will float up to heaven (or down to hell) at death. This is a very primitive notion and one that has been abandoned by more advanced theological thinkers.

The soul is not a thing that you own, but an expression of your personality, or a form of consciousness. But, when does one become an individualized soul? When does God "breathe the breath of life" into a person? When does this universal consciousness arrive at a point where we call it a soul? People have tried to answer this question in a number of ways, and it has even been angrily debated by the United States Congress on the abortion issue. Some say it is about five months after conception when the fetus takes its first breath in the mother's womb; it moves and its heart beats. Some say it occurs after about three months when the embryo is fully formed. Others insist that the soul is present at the very moment of conception, and still others say the soul appears when the baby is born and takes his or her first breath of fresh air.

What is the answer to this dilemma? The problem is that the question is phrased incorrectly. The soul is not "born" at some particular moment in time because it is not a fixed state of being but a state of *becoming*. Soul is synonymous with personality, representing the conscious part of it. Therefore, it is not something that leaps into the baby's body at some historical point, but something that gradually emerges as the child matures. If we want to use the word *born*, we would say that the soul is born when *self*-consciousness appears, for this is the main attribute of the soul. Until this occurs, the soul exists only in potential. When a human baby is born, it is on much the same plane as the animal, for it is not a fully developed, distinct personality until it has awareness of itself as an individual; that is, when self-consciousness has developed. Up to that point we might say that a newborn baby is a latent soul, or an expression of pure Spirit. It is the same way that a seed in the ground has the potentiality to become a flower, and eventually it will burst its shell and a shoot will appear. But we don't call it a tulip until we can see the budding of the flower.

The child's soul, or personality, develops as a result of the interaction of two factors: its inherited characteristics and environment. This interaction produces behavior, and it is this behavior, which includes cognitive processes, that we call personality. Before this interaction begins, usually between one and two years of age, the child has only the potential for "self"-consciousness, because it doesn't have awareness of itself. Maturation over a period of time is required for the emergence of a structured personality, and the full development of the soul.

Most people realize their full potentiality only upon reaching early adulthood, because the full development of the soul necessarily depends upon the acquisition of two important human attributes: rational thought and abstract verbal skills. If these two abilities don't develop properly, the person will have a very restrained, limited, and restricted personality, or expression of soul. As Barbara Branden stated in her lecture on Efficient Thinking: "Language is the only form in which it is possible to reason explicitly, and to subject one's conclusions to the judgment of reason and reality. In order to think, man has to draw abstractions, to form concepts, and to give these concepts identity by means of specific words." In the case of people who are mute, these words are in the symbolic form of signs that convey meaning, rather than words.

Our definition of the soul is this: It is *the individual's unique organization of inherited characteristics and environmental influences.* The mixture of these two factors results in consistent behavioral patterns whereby we can identify and relate to others. Our behavior is more or less the same (within a certain range) as we go about our daily life, and this consistency, which we call our personality, is the result of our genetics and environment. Environment includes not only the type of parenting we had as a child, but also social and cultural factors. The soul is the organizing function within the individual, and the means by which one human being can relate to another. So the soul is not a possession nor a thing; it is not a constant, or fixed entity, because it is always growing, changing, and evolving.

The soul is that aspect of your consciousness that can originate ideas, think, make decisions, and reason. It is the *individualized* aspect of Spirit and is therefore different in everyone. Spirit is the *universal* aspect of the personality and is the same in everyone. Soul represents our sense of personal self-identity as it expresses itself uniquely through each person. Although Spirit Within is constant and operates in basically the same way within each individual, each soul is different, because every person has a different genetic and environmental history (see Figure 3, page 28).

In the development of the human brain we now have for the first time in evolutionary history the division of consciousness into two parts. Consciousness is no longer singular, as it is in the lower phases of the evolutionary continuum, because humans have a dual nature. Consciousness manifests in us as soul and Spirit, or the conscious and subconscious minds. Reflective thought, a uniquely human ability, requires that division of consciousness, for one aspect must be able to reflect upon the other. Logic and reason are the predominant characteristics of the conscious mind, and emotion and intuition are those of the subconscious. These different aspects have their separate physiological correlates in the right and left hemispheres of the brain, and function oppositionally.

Another point is that the soul must always have some form through which to express itself, and that form on this plane of existence is the physical body. We can only recognize other people because they are expressing themselves through a physical medium; otherwise, they would have no personality or existence. Form is an attribute of consciousness, and all manifestations of consciousness have form. Does this mean, then, that the soul is gone once the physical body is gone? No, but it does mean that the soul must express itself through some other form, otherwise it would have no continuing existence. In metaphysics this other form is called the astral or etheric body, which it is said we possess along with the physical body.

Now that we are in the universe, a part of us is here forever, because the Law of Conservation of Energy states that energy

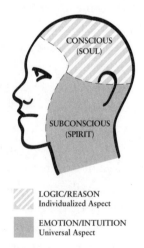

Figure 3.
Relationship of Soul
to Spirit.

can neither be created nor destroyed; it can only change form. Matter and consciousness are indestructible. When we die, the atoms of our physical bodies merely return to the earth and change form, but our self-consciousness, and Spirit within us which is a part of the All, continues its evolutionary process on other planes. Nothing is ever gone forever.

We must realize that soul and body do not act as separate entities. The organism functions as a single unity, and what happens to a part always affects the whole. Every thought we think produces an immediate physiological response, for the relationship between soul and body is intimate in the extreme. The body is certainly a part of our personality, the most evident part. We would have no self-identity without our physical identity. Certainly, our self-image is greatly influenced by the condition of our physical medium.

Souls, or personalities, are at different stages of development. Some are very advanced, others are very deficient and functioning at a minimal level. Not all adults achieve full maturity. Some remain almost infantile in their expression, and we could say that they have a restricted personality, or a limited soul development. Many people are not even remotely aware of their higher nature as they rush through life operating by conditioned reflex, just like an animal. Such people never raise their consciousness much above that of the beast, and the spark of divinity within them remains dormant for the whole of their lives.

It is the task of each of us to awaken the divine spark within, thereby attaining individual consciousness first, and secondly, unity with Spirit. That is what being a soul really means. It may seem incredible that some people have not yet reached individual consciousness, but this is actually their level of development. They are entirely reactive beings; they have very little free will because they just give programmed responses to environmental stimuli, without thinking or reasoning about their reactions. They are little more than talking animals, and they live out their lives largely unconsciously. Sometimes their subconscious mind, which is always striving toward expansion, has to totally disrupt the limited lives of such people in order to force them to grow.

The great task of our lives, and the duty of every man and woman, is to work at increasing our self-awareness and freeing ourselves from the enslavement of past conditioning. It is our responsibility to become aware of the fact that we are a part of the Infinite, and to begin expressing this higher consciousness through our personalities. It is only when there is some measure of synthesis established between the conscious and subconscious aspects of an individual's being that he or she begins to establish a true identity as a person and becomes a soul. Only then is a person fully awakened.

In our unconscious mind we cannot
distinguish between a wish and a deed.

SIGMUND FREUD

THREE

Reprogramming Your Mind

Soul and Spirit, conscious
and subconscious mind: how do these two aspects of
mankind's dual nature interact? How do we get programmed to the various concepts that govern our
lives, and how can we reprogram our minds to eliminate negative ideas so that we may live happily and
productively?

Of course Spirit flows through both aspects, but it
is partially shut off from our conscious awareness by
what we will call a *psychic barrier,* or psychic censor,
preventing us from having complete contact with our
subconscious. But this barrier is permeable, like a sieve
that a person might use to sift flour, because the soul
can never operate entirely independent of Spirit, and
its manifestation is always the result of the interaction

between the two parts. Because this barrier isn't solid, we often get messages from our inner self, in the form of intuitive insights, dreams, or precognition of events.

It is because this psychic barrier exists that individuality is possible. If this division of consciousness were not there, we would all be the same and have no distinct personality, nor self-awareness. Certain differences in temperament would exist, as they do in the animal world, due to genetic predispositions, but there would not be a sense of identity, a self-image, or rational thinking, all of which are aspects of our personality.

As stated earlier, soul is the individualized aspect of our personality, the part that originates the ideas that will manifest in our life, or accepts these ideas from others. These concepts then lodge in our subconscious mind, and it is the subconscious that carries them out. Soul, therefore, is the *thinker*. It can also be considered the originative, "masculine" aspect of the self, because it accepts ideas from the environment, and implants them in the subconscious mind.

Spirit, the subconscious, is the *doer*, the receptive, "feminine" aspect, since it receives the ideas from the conscious part of the mind and proceeds to carry them out. (This division is the same whether a person is male or female.) As a comparison, in the world of labor, soul is the foreman, and Spirit the laborer who carries out the orders. To use a technology metaphor, Spirit is the hardware part of the computer that has the motherboard, and soul is the software that you program to tell it what you want it to do. If you want to write a letter, you use a word processing program but, if you want to keep track of your investments, then you will install a financial program that has a spreadsheet. It's the same creative principle at work in the realm of the mind as in the biological world: the masculine, originative soul impregnates the feminine, receptive Spirit with an idea, and the creation that results from this interaction is the physical expression, or behavior.

Let's say the soul looks out the window and, seeing that it's a pleasant day, originates the idea of going for a walk. It can consciously think up this idea, but actually has no power to carry it out since it doesn't know which muscles are involved in the simple act of taking a step. For instance, if you wanted to get up from a chair and had to do it using only your conscious mind, you wouldn't be able to do so. In fact, we're not even aware of which muscles we use first in the simple act of rising from a chair. We've all seen pictures on television of the enormous difficulty a disabled person has in learning to walk again. He or she has to be taught which muscles to move in order to take a step, and it's a laborious process when done with the conscious mind. What we normally do without being aware of it, is turn our idea over to Spirit, the receptive, formative aspect of our personality, which then activates the many muscles involved. Walking is the behavior that results from this interchange.

Definition of Mind

We have discussed the subconscious and the conscious aspects of our personality, but what is mind? Although we must necessarily use the word "mind" as though it were a noun, it's actually not a thing; it is a function, a process; it has no existence in and of itself. Mind is a term used to describe the action of the cells, neurons, synapses, and chemical processes of the brain. It is the information-processing activity of the brain. Mind is simply the name we have given to the *interaction* between soul and Spirit— the process of thinking. Mind, therefore, is not like the soul, which is the organizing factor within the personality and is an entity in itself. But the mind is a temporary, fleeting phenomenon dependent entirely upon stimuli from the internal and external environment. Since it is not a thing but a process, it really should be a verb, such as "minding," rather than a noun (see Figure 4, following page).

In order for the process of thinking to occur, an impression must be transmitted to the soul, which we receive through one or more of our five senses, and that information is automatically transmitted to Spirit Within. To understand how this works, we must accept the scientific theory that we actually don't see, hear, smell, taste, or touch "things," but everything in the universe is really a vibration or a certain wavelength, which our brain interprets as a particular object or sensation. For example, you look out your window and see the neighbor's cat lounging on the front lawn. Spirit matches that visual impression with one of the patterns in its vast data bank and flashes that back to the soul, which is then able to interpret the particular vibration (or wavelength) that it has picked up through its perceptual senses, as a cat. This interaction between conscious and subconscious is instantaneous, of course, and is the process we call thinking.

According to science, what occurs is that the firing of certain neurons in the brain reaches a "critical level of awareness," which causes a person to become conscious of a particular vibration. She then translates that vibration according to what-

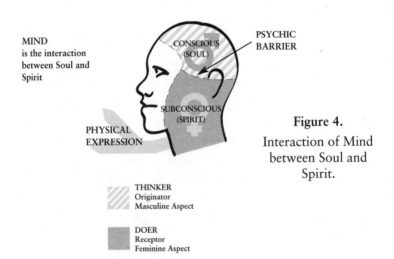

MIND
is the interaction
between Soul and
Spirit

CONSCIOUS
(SOUL)

PSYCHIC
BARRIER

SUBCONSCIOUS
(SPIRIT)

PHYSICAL
EXPRESSION

THINKER
Originator
Masculine Aspect

DOER
Receptor
Feminine Aspect

Figure 4.
Interaction of Mind
between Soul and
Spirit.

ever is in her memory bank that resonates to it. Each part of the brain is always at a certain level of alertness. There are always some neurons firing somewhere in the brain, even when we're sleeping. The cells are in a constant state of vibration. When certain neurons fire above a specific critical level, the neural processes are consciously experienced, and we have a thought about something. We could say that the amplitude, or strength, of the vibration of particular cells and neurons increases when coming in contact with stimuli that resonates to their particular vibration, and we become consciously aware of it. Mind is the name given to this activity of the brain cells; therefore it is that portion of your consciousness above a critical level of alertness or vibration at a given time. When you are asleep none of your brain cells are vibrating above this level and, therefore, you are not consciously aware of anything.

Let's say you're strolling down Main Street and pass a bakery. Stimuli will be received through your olfactory sense, or sense of smell. At that moment you pick up a vibration that will be in resonance with certain cells of your brain related to that stimuli, and neurons will begin firing. When their amplitude (or volume) becomes heightened above a critical level, you will have a thought that there is fresh bread baking in that store, and then you will have to decide whether or not to go into the store and buy some.

Every experience we have ever had is impressed somewhere on electrochemical cells in our brain. This is our storehouse of memory, akin to an enormous data bank. Every time the soul is consciously aware of a stimulus the subconscious instantly activates its storage system, and fires the associated brain neurons to identify the experience so that you can interpret it for what it is. In the 1930s, Dr. Wilder Penfield, a Canadian neurosurgeon, performed some interesting experiments at McGill University in Montreal, during open-brain surgery on his patients. As he touched the cerebellum of the conscious patient with electrodes, he asked them to report what they experienced. They reported remarkably vivid memories, and the smallest shift of the stimulant would generate distinctly separate thoughts. Penfield mapped the location of each memory as he scanned the brain with his probe and, whenever he went back to that particular location, the same memory would reappear.* In Penfield's account of a young woman, he stated, "she had the same 'flashback' several times. These had to do with her cousin's house, or the trip there . . . a trip she had not made for about fifteen years, but made often as a child." This experiment proved that the brain is a fabulous recording device, and everything we have ever seen, heard, smelled, touched, or tasted is imprinted on our brain cells forever. Whenever something reactivates those cells, we get a mental picture duplicating the original experience, although it may be somewhat distorted because of the accompanying emotions at the time.

But what happens if you hear about, or see, something of which you have no knowledge? Since an impression has been registered on the cells of your brain, Spirit will simply provide you with a related, or associated picture, based on past programming so that you can make a determination of what it is, or what it is similar to. In essence, it's an educated guess.

How Our Minds Become Programmed

Only the conscious part of the "mind" has the ability to distinguish between constructive and destructive ideas, an ability not always used wisely, for too often people unwittingly originate or accept negative concepts that eventually will impact or control their lives.

Let's begin the process of reprogramming our mind to constructive thoughts by examining the way negative concepts lodge in our subconscious. An understanding of this will enable you to

---

* Kelly, Kevin. *Out of Control*, Addison-Wesley, N.Y., 1994.

reprogram Spirit with the concepts you want in your life, and to eliminate negative ones you may have already acquired.

Inductive Reasoning and Deduction

The conscious part of our mind has two types of processes available to it: induction and deduction. The subconscious, on the other hand, is more limited and can only use one process: deduction. This fact is of enormous importance in understanding how the mind works, because these processes operate quite differently (Figure 5, below).

Inductive reasoning, *solely* a function of the conscious mind, involves analyzing, judging, and selecting, as when you assemble a number of disparate ideas and compare them. This involves *thinking,* a function *only* of the conscious mind. For example, when you enter a meeting room, you choose a place to sit by using inductive reasoning. You may want to sit by a window, or near a friend, or in a comfortable chair, or close to the speaker. You examine the possibilities, analyze them, and select the one that best suits your criteria. This is induction and obviously involves thinking.

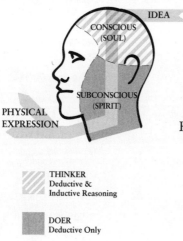

Figure 5.
Functions of Conscious
and Subconscious
Aspects.

Deductive functioning, which does not involve reasoning, can also be used by the conscious mind, but it is the *only* method available to the subconscious. This fact is tremendously important for reprogramming the subconscious because deduction doesn't involve thinking. It simply accepts the ideas or premises given to it, and then draws a conclusion from them. Right or wrong, it doesn't matter to the subconscious. The evidence that the subconscious mind functions deductively is dramatically demonstrated through hypnosis. In this altered state of consciousness, a hypnotist talks directly to the subconscious mind of a subject without interference from the rational, conscious portion, which has been temporarily suspended.

As has been well documented, in the hypnotic state, subjects can produce phenomena that would be difficult, if not impossible, during their normal, fully conscious state. They have, for example, been observed to maintain cataleptic postures for hours without discomfort, to enjoy a glass of vinegar thinking it's tea, and to have needles stuck in their flesh without bleeding or feeling pain, among other unusual phenomena. These abnormal effects are produced because, in hypnosis, the subconscious of the subject accepts the suggestions of the hypnotist without reasoning or questioning them, testifying to the receptive, passive, unquestioning, nonanalytical, deductive nature of the subconscious mind.

In order to reprogram our minds to positive concepts, we must have an understanding of how Spirit, or the subconscious, operates. Generally speaking, deduction starts with given premises, and leads to a conclusion. A premise is simply a statement; it can be true or false. Two premises, a major and a minor one, plus a conclusion deduced from them, form what is know in logic and metaphysics as a syllogism. The conclusion is colored, of course, by whether the premises are true or not, but the important point is that a conclusion can only be drawn from the given data.

Here is a classic example of a syllogism:

Major premise: All trees have roots.

Minor premise: An oak is a tree.

Therefore: An oak has roots.

There is no thinking involved in this process. It's just the logical deduction from the given premises, and this is exactly how our subconscious operates.

When the soul originates certain premises, or accepts them from others (such as a parent), it turns them over to Spirit, which draws a conclusion and operates on the basis of that conclusion, whether the premises are true or false. Since Spirit cannot judge the accuracy of the premises or reject them if they are false, it has no choice but to accept and implement them. Obviously, if you give your subconscious false premises, you will get an erroneous conclusion, which will eventually manifest in your life. If you give Spirit premises that are harmful or destructive to you, you will be harmed or even eventually destroyed by the conclusion you force it to act out. Remember, *Spirit cannot reason*—that is solely an ability of the conscious mind.

Let's look at a few samples of injurious syllogisms that are so commonplace we often incorporate them into our subconscious without thinking about the consequences.

Major premise: My father had a heart attack.

Minor premise: I am just like my father.

Therefore: I will have a heart attack.

Major premise: Mommy says I'm stupid.

Minor premise: Mommy is always right.

Therefore: I'm stupid.

Major premise: If you get your feet wet,
    you'll catch a cold.

Minor premise: My feet are wet.

Therefore: I will catch a cold.

Major premise: Women can't earn a lot of money.

Minor premise: I'm a woman.

Therefore: I can't earn a lot of money.

This is how negative concepts are programmed into the subconscious mind, and Spirit has no choice but to carry them out, no matter how harmful they are. Because of the importance of this truth, always remember that Spirit cannot reason upon your ideas. It has no ability to analyze or evaluate them, but can only accept your orders, constructive or destructive. Therefore, *correct programming of the mind must begin at the conscious level.*

Your personality is much like a highly sophisticated computer. Except for automatic biological processes, the soul is the programmer and must program data into the subconscious before it can receive output. In order for the deductive process to begin, the subconscious must be given input in the form of premises, which are the data it receives from the soul. These premises are ideas that you originate yourself, or ones that you accept from others, such as your parents, teachers, clergy, partner, and even advertisers in print and broadcast media. If, therefore, your life is a mess, *you* ordered it! Either you programmed your subconscious with negative ideas, or someone else did it for you, and now it's manifesting in your life. But, understanding how the personality functions, you can reverse the process and reprogram your subconscious mind to the positive ideas that will make your life successful and fulfilling!

You may be wondering how Spirit, which cannot reason and originate ideas, can give you direction and guide your life. You must ask it for help first. You have to tune into it, and then it will respond. Spirit doesn't need to originate answers for you; it already has all the answers in the great storehouse of wisdom that psychiatrist Carl Jung called "the Collective Unconscious." When you are ready and know how to ask for it, it will select the appropriate answer, and present it to you in the form of intuitive insights, visions, or dreams.

Understanding how the mind functions, we must be very careful about the ideas we allow to become lodged in our subconscious. If you are wise, you will learn to keep eternal vigil over your soul in order to reject the myriad negative ideas with which we are all constantly bombarded. And, if you now have a number of negative concepts lodged in your subconscious disturbing your life, you will find that the techniques for transformation covered in the remaining chapters will help you to dislodge them. You have the power within you right now to reprogram those ideas and create for yourself whatever type of life you want!

PART TWO

Techniques for
Transformation

Only when people realize that they have the
power to use their thoughts to lift themselves
from misery; only then will their freedom begin.

DR. THURMAN FLEET, *Concept-Therapy*

The cure of the soul has to be effected by the use of certain charms, and these charms are fair words.

Socrates

FOUR
Self-Hypnosis: The Magic Doorway

One of the fastest ways to tap the great power of your inner mind is through self-hypnosis—a doorway to the tremendous storehouse of your subconscious wisdom. There is no power in the world as great as the forces in your own mind, and self-hypnosis is a direct pipeline through which you can release these powers. The person who learns the technique of self-hypnosis has discovered the secret of successful living, thus it is important that you understand hypnosis in order to use self-hypnosis most effectively.

Many people still have some very confused notions about hypnosis because of the classic fictional portrait of a bearded Svengali with his long black cape, making weird passes over the helpless subject, Trilby.

Unfortunately, it is true that some stage hypnotists have perverted the purpose of hypnosis by using it to make people bark like dogs or cluck like chickens, and generally make fools of themselves. Occasionally amateurs, after learning a few basic principles of hypnosis, use it to show off at parties, and may cause harm by giving their subjects detrimental suggestions.

The danger is not in hypnosis *per se,* but in the application of it. Hypnosis is extremely beneficial because it is a state of very deep relaxation. In the hands of a trained professional, hypnosis can alleviate insomnia, reduce anxiety, facilitate weight loss, help overcome bad habits, and improve our lives in a great many ways. Hypnosis has an essential place in psychotherapy, where it can be used to enhance the therapeutic process, and in surgery and dentistry, where it is used for pain relief. Under hypnosis you will feel totally relaxed, calm, and peaceful, an altered state extremely beneficial to your body. Hypnosis will help you get in touch with the most profound part of your nature, the subconscious mind.

Hypnosis doesn't necessarily mean that someone has to be in a trance, as you might think of a trance state. It is merely an extension of common states of mind, of the everyday trances all of us have from time to time when we become deeply absorbed in reverie, or preoccupied with something, oblivious to what is happening around us.

We see waking hypnosis around us every day. It is not some strange, mysterious thing limited to abnormal conditions, but a daily occurrence for all of us. In its most elementary form it's called salesmanship; in its most profound form it can save your life. Have you ever been driving your car down the freeway and discovered you passed the exit you wanted? That's because you were in a mild hypnotic trance, deeply absorbed in thought. Or, have you ever driven through a town and later didn't remember having gone through it? That's hypnotic amnesia. We drive both consciously and subconsciously. It has become such a habit that the conscious mind can be totally engaged in talking or thinking while the subconscious keeps the car on the road. Typists are familiar with this phenomenon. One can be typing material while his or her mind is engaged in thinking of several different things, because it is partly done unconsciously.

Hypnosis is simply a state of heightened suggestibility. It doesn't necessarily involve closing your eyes and going into a trance. Any time you accept a suggestion from someone else, that's a form of hypnosis. For instance, if I say: "You should wear your raincoat today because I think it's going to rain," and you do it, that's a form of mild hypnosis because you have accepted my suggestion.

Human life could not go on without the use of hypnosis because, if no one ever accepted a suggestion from someone else, nothing would happen. Corporations pay huge fees to advertising agencies, which know the art of getting others to accept suggestions. Television commercials are filled with ideas that flow in such rapid succession, and in so many attractive forms, that observers don't have the opportunity to use their reason; thus, the suggestions become lodged in the subconscious mind. Whenever you go out and buy a product you have seen advertised, you are responding to a hypnotic suggestion. Life would be very limited without the power of suggestion, but it is a matter of learning to accept the right suggestions—the ideas that we want to see manifested in our lives, and also dehypnotizing ourselves to the negative suggestions we have already accepted.

Contrary to popular belief, no one can hypnotize you if you are unwilling because, in the final analysis, all hypnosis is self-hypnosis. No one has any special power that you do not possess yourself. A hypnotist is merely a person who has learned a technique for helping you to contact your own subconscious mind. But you must be willing to go along with the suggestions, or they won't work. If you are willing to play the part of the subject and allow someone else to play the part of the operator, you can be hypnotized. The ability to be hypnotized is not some mysterious, magical thing; it's really very easy and simple, and anyone who is willing to try can achieve it. Hypnosis is a matter of degree. Some people make excellent subjects right from the beginning and can go very deeply into the trance state, but others may require some training. Hypnosis is a learned ability; if you wish to become a good subject, you can be trained to achieve a deep trance state. The important thing to remember is that *the power to be hypnotized does not lie with the hypnotist; it lies with the subject.*

Hypnosis is imagination, not willpower. It's not a matter of domination or being weak-willed. Hypnosis is a matter of concentration and the willingness to accept suggestions, and has nothing whatsoever to do with willpower. In fact, highly intelligent, creative people tend to be the best hypnotic subjects. Doctors Ernest and Josephine Hilgard, through research in the Psychology department at Stanford University, discovered that university students who have a history of, and a capability for, a high degree of imaginative involvement make excellent subjects. "By imaginative involvement," say the Hilgards, "is meant an absorption in some kind of fantasy so real that ordinary reality is set aside; the experience is felt as actually being lived, and is savored as such. The scientist who enjoys science fiction, without any detriment to his or her career as a critical scientist, furnishes an illustration of this flexibility. The areas of involvement differ from person to person, such as reading, music, religion, an aesthetic interest in nature, extensive daydreaming, some forms of physical activity, such as skiing, skin-diving, cave-exploring, any of these areas may provide a preparation for and a path into hypnotic experience." Creative people, who have highly developed imaginations, are excellent subjects for hypnosis. Youngsters are also very responsive to hypnosis because their imagination is less restrained and rigid than their elders.

Most people find self-hypnosis relatively easy to master, but others require more practice. It may be helpful for you to be put into a hypnotic trance by a professional person first because, once the state has been experienced, it's easier to do it yourself. Although people fear giving up control to another person, the fact is that hypnosis will not rob you of your willpower, nor diminish your self-control. No one can force you to be hypnotized, nor can he or she make you do something under hypnosis that you don't want to do. If you are told to do something that is objectionable to you, you will simply sit there and do nothing, or you will open your eyes and come out of the trance.

I once told a man under hypnosis that the glass of water I handed him was a caffeinated soft drink. His eyes remained closed, but he would not take a sip of the water. He later revealed that he was a member of a church that did not allow drinking any beverage containing caffeine. There is something operating within us that protects us from acting on suggestions that are contrary to our nature; otherwise, we would buy every product that advertisers pitch on television. Even so, you should never allow yourself to be hypnotized by a person who does not fully understand the incredible forces that are being dealt with under hypnosis. If you seek help for an emotional problem, carefully check the background and credentials of the hypnotist, who should be someone licensed in the healing arts, such as a psychologist, psychiatrist, marriage and family counselor (certified in some states, such as California, to practice hypnosis), or clinical social worker.

Contrary to popular belief, there is no loss of consciousness in hypnosis. The subject is actually acutely aware, even in the deepest stages. If the demonstration is before a group, the subject is conscious of the fact that he or she is being observed. During a class demonstration, a hypnotist once placed me in a state of catalepsy in order to be suspended in a horizontal position between two chairs, my body supported only by my head and feet. I had just had my hair styled in a French bun that morning, and one of the men who lifted my rigid body into position accidentally knocked my head and ruined the hairstyle. I was wholly aware of this—and was a little disturbed by it—but it didn't interfere with the trance.

It is often difficult for most people to tell when they have achieved the hypnotic state. The transition from the conscious to the trance state is so gradual, and the psychological and physiological evidence of change so subtle, it is practically impossible, especially when using self-hypnosis, to determine which state exists at any given moment. It is entirely possible for a person to go into a trance with one's eyes wide open—and remain open during the trance. It is certainly possible to talk, although one's speech is usually slowed down. Some individuals experience sensations in hypnosis such as floating, disassociation from their bodies, lightheadedness, tingling, heaviness of the limbs, and so forth; but others notice very little difference. For example, I have hypnotized people to stop smoking who felt nothing had actually taken place during the session, and thought the hypnosis hadn't worked, but who never smoked another cigarette again.

Another myth is that a hypnotized person is asleep. Although the induction procedure usually contains such suggestions as "you are feeling very sleepy and tired," what the subject achieves is a "sleep-resembling" state, but not actual sleep. The subject has to be sufficiently awake to hear the instructions of the hypnotist and, if he or she actually falls asleep, the instructions will not be carried out. Although the muscles are loose and relaxed during hypnosis, the brain is acutely concentrated, and the subject focuses on what the hypnotist says to a very high degree. Occasionally, the subject will go into a light sleep under hypnosis. Studies have shown that hypnosis is still effective because the suggestions of the hypnotist will go directly into the subject's subconscious mind. If imagery work is used, however, such as having an overweight woman imagine herself slim, it is better for the subject to be awake to participate in the visualization.

Another misconception about hypnosis is that there is a complete loss of memory of everything that has occurred while in a trance. This happens very infrequently and usually only when the hypnotist has given the subject the direct suggestion that there will be amnesia regarding what has taken place. Under ordinary circumstances, a subject is aware of everything that is said, and able to recall it.

One of the great fears of many people is that they will reveal all their deep, dark secrets under hypnosis. Since hypnotic subjects are completely aware of their surroundings, they would no more betray a confidence, or embarrass themselves, than if they were wide awake in front of the same people. Subjects do not volunteer information under hypnosis; if a question should prove embarrassing, they will simply sit there and say nothing. An alert hypnotist will spot the resistance and change the suggestion.

People often wonder what would happen if the hypnotist dies, or walks away and never comes back while a subject is under hypnosis? Though this is extremely unlikely, the subject will merely awaken spontaneously when ready. Very infrequently, a subject will not open his or her eyes when instructed to do so by the hypnotist. This is no cause for alarm; usually the person is simply tired and enjoying the rest. Given the suggestion that five minutes of hypnotic "sleep" is equal to five hours of real sleep, the person will awaken completely refreshed after five minutes. Or, the subject can simply be allowed to awaken whenever he or she wants. In self-hypnosis, you will give yourself a prearranged signal to awaken at a certain time, or after counting to a certain number.

The secret involved in hypnosis, including self-hypnosis, is an inner agreement with one's self. You must consciously cooperate in the process and be as open and receptive as possible. If you are thinking: "This isn't going to work," you lessen the efficacy of the process. If, on the other hand, you completely accept that you are going to be successful, your subconscious mind will accept it also. Affirming to yourself that what is being suggested is really happening, leads to conviction.

A trained hypnotist is able to determine how deeply hypnotized a subject is by observing the bodily signs carefully, or by making certain tests, such as locking the subject's fingers together or questioning him or her with prearranged finger signals. Certain phenomena are characteristic of each of the three basic stages of hypnosis, although individual responses may vary.

Lethargy is the first and lightest stage of hypnosis, characterized by muscular relaxation and dormancy of the senses.

The second stage is *Catalepsy.* It is usually produced by a sharp clap of the hands or another kind of loud noise in the ears of a lethargic subject. In this state the subject is characterized by a statuesque immobility. The muscles are rigid, not relaxed, and will remain in the most difficult postures for hours without apparent fatigue. Hypnotists who perform for entertainment often demonstrate this stage by stretching the subject across the top of two chairs, suspended by only the back of their neck and ankles. Then, to prove that it's not just playacting, they have one or two people sit on the subject's stomach, and they will remain rigid.

Somnambulism is the deepest stage of hypnosis. This state results in an increased activity of the senses. It is the stage at which the wonders of hypnosis manifest. People are able to produce phenomena that they could not possibly duplicate while in their normal, waking state. These are such phenomena as tremendous feats of memory, super strength, acuity in hearing, etc., sometimes reported in the news media. For example, you may have heard about the 110-pound mother who lifted a Volkswagen with one hand and pulled her trapped son from beneath it with the other hand. Under normal conditions she would have been incapable of this kind of strength, but at that moment of panic her rational mind could not tell her she was unable to lift a car, so she tapped directly into her subconscious mind and found the ability inherent within her. This was a state of self-induced hypnosis. This is what hypnosis demonstrates: that there are virtually limitless capabilities within all of us if we only learn how to tap the wisdom of the subconscious mind.

The reason hypnosis works is because of the following four principles:

1. Imagination is more powerful than willpower.

In any battle between the will and the imagination, the imagination always wins. If you imagine something under hypnosis, even though your reason is telling you it isn't so, you will produce the effect. Using this principle, you should employ your imagination, not your reason, if you want to achieve something. For instance, if you want to lose a few pounds and are offered a delicious dish of ice cream, you should immediately imagine how attractive and happy you will be when you reach your weight goal, rather than trying to use willpower to argue against accepting the dessert. If, instead, you begin to imagine how good the ice cream will taste, and then attempt to use your willpower to resist the temptation, you will be defeated.

2. Imagination is more powerful than reason.

This principle has led many normal, rational people to blindly follow a despot or dictator because their imagination overpowered their reason. This is why the con artist is successful: he or she manipulates people's imagination. It is also why we sometimes fall in love with someone our reason tells us is totally wrong for us, but something about them has captured our imagination (our fantasy), and we are overcome by it.

3. Only one idea can be entertained by the mind at any given time.

If a hypnotist tells you that your hands are stuck tightly together, either you must affirm to yourself that they are, or think: "No, they are not." Conflicting ideas cannot be held at one and the same time, thus, to be successful in hypnosis, you must not resist the suggestion given.

4. Any imagined condition will become real if persisted in, provided only that it is logical.

The subconscious mind cannot tell the difference between an idea that is strongly imagined and something actually happening in the outer world. That is why hypnosis and imaging work. After the hypnotic suggestion has incubated, it will begin to manifest itself in your life, provided only that the suggestion is logical.

Inducing Self-Hypnosis

The first requirement for inducing self-hypnosis is to get into a relaxed position. Sit in a comfortable chair, hands loosely on your lap, legs uncrossed, and feet flat on the floor. Adjust any uncomfortable clothing, such as a tight belt. Focus your eyes on a point near the ceiling. Almost any object will do, but be sure it is above eye level since this puts a small strain on the eyes and makes it easier to close them. As you focus on this object, say to yourself: "My eyelids are becoming heavier and heavier. Soon they will be so heavy that they will close, and I will be totally relaxed." Pay close attention to your eyelids and, as you repeat the sentences to yourself, you will feel the desire to close your eyes. Don't resist the urge; just allow your eyes to close when you are ready.

As an alternative, you can count from one to ten, closing your eyes on the even numbers and opening them on the odd ones. Your eyes should stay closed by the time you get to ten; if not, simply begin your count again. As your eyes close, it is a good idea to use a key phrase, such as "relax now," to deepen the state. This phrase should be repeated very slowly three times. This will become your trigger for inducing the state again and should be used each time. If you wish, you can use the "Relaxation Process" in Appendix A (see page 205) to bring your entire body into a state of deep relaxation after you close your eyes by putting this suggestion on tape, and playing it while relaxing.

The next step is to choose a way to induce increased, deep muscular relaxation. A common image used by hypnotists is the suggestion of going down in an elevator, while counting the floors from one to ten. If you are afraid of elevators, you can use an escalator or staircase. I usually find, however, that by giving the suggestion to subjects that "this is a very safe elevator, perfectly safe in every way," even those who dislike elevators are not averse to riding it in their imagination. You can count the floors one to ten, or backwards from ten to one, just as though you were going down into the basement of a large department store. The idea of going down into the subconscious is a universally used symbol. Going up symbolizes the conscious mind; going down is, of course, associated with going deeper.

As you begin your slow descent and accompanying count of the floors you pass, repeat phrases to yourself that indicate relaxing, getting sleepy and tired, going deeper and deeper. In your mind's eye, see the numbers on the elevator indicator taking you further and further down. When you arrive at the bottom floor, imagine the elevator door opening to a room that has a big, soft, comfortable bed in it. You walk over to the bed, stretch out on it, and go into a hypnotic sleep. As you lie down on the bed, say to yourself: "I am now in a very pleasant hypnotic sleep, and I will stay in this state until I come back up the elevator." (Or, until you count to ten, or until whatever prearranged signal.)

You will now be at least lightly in hypnosis and, after practice, will be able to achieve a deep state. If you feel that you are not completely relaxed while lying in the bed, imagine some other scene of relaxation—lying on the grass under a tree on a warm, summer day, or sitting by a placid lake, or even relaxing in a hot bath. Use any image that conveys to you the idea of becoming more deeply relaxed.

While you are in a state of hypnosis, time may seem to pass very quickly. Sometimes it seems as though you've been in the state for an hour or so although it's actually only been fifteen minutes. You may even drop off into a light sleep if you are tired. You can avoid this by taking a sitting, not reclining, position and by giving yourself suggestions that you will remain awake. It is crucial to be awake in self-hypnosis because you have to give yourself suggestions. You can also give yourself a posthypnotic suggestion that you will awaken fully at a specific time so that you control the length of time you remain under hypnosis. This is the technique many people use to nap for exactly half an hour, and always wake up at the designated time.

In your initial sessions, you must allow yourself at least a half-hour for induction and suggestions. After you become proficient at self-hypnosis, you should be able to put yourself under in as little as five minutes, then take another ten minutes or so for your suggestions.

After you have given yourself the suggestion that you are now in a hypnotic sleep, test the depth of the hypnotic state, and practice accepting a suggestion you make to yourself. A good initial test is the "stuck eyelids test." With your eyes closed, say to yourself: "I am going to count to five; at the count of five, my eyelids will be stuck tightly together, and I will be unable to open them until I am ready to wake up." Then repeat something similar to the following:

1. My eyelids are now sticking tightly together, and I am unable to open them.
2. The harder I try, the tighter the lids will stick together.

3. My eyelids are now stuck tightly together, just as though there were a thick, heavy glue on them locking them together; and I cannot open my eyes until I'm ready to come out of my hypnotic state.

4. In a moment I am going to try to open my eyelids, but I will not be able to do so because they are locked so tightly together. It is impossible to open them; the harder I try, the more they resist.

5. Tight, tight, locked tight; and I cannot open my eyes until I am ready to wake up.

Now, try to open your eyes. If the test is successful, your eyelids will stay closed no matter how hard you try to open them. The principle involved here is that you cannot think two conflicting thoughts at the same time. As long as you strongly believe that you cannot open your eyes, it will be quite impossible to open them. In accepting your suggestion, your subconscious blocks the nerve impulses from reaching the muscles of your eyelids, so they will not move.

Some people may not like to use this test since the thought of not being able to open their eyes is frightening, even though they're in control. If you feel this way, use a similar test, the "hand-clasp test." Before entering hypnosis, interlock your fingers in a comfortable position in your lap. After the induction process, give yourself the same type of suggestions used for stuck eyelids, but substitute "stuck hands." As you lock your hands together, squeeze your palms tightly, and visualize a thick, heavy glue locking them in this position. Either of these tests will deepen hypnosis.

If you fail the test, give yourself further suggestions to deepen the relaxation, such as, "As I lie here relaxing, I am going deeper and deeper and becoming more and more relaxed. Physical comfort exists, and my subconscious mind has slowed down my breathing and pulse rate as I relax even deeper. I am becoming an excellent hypnotic subject, and my subconscious mind is responding to all my suggestions. Now I am drifting down more and more rapidly and becoming more drowsy and tired. I am now going into a very pleasant hypnotic sleep." You can also use a hand signal, such as saying to yourself: "When my index finger rises, I will then be in a deep hypnotic trance." Then wait for your subconscious mind to carry out this order.

Once you are in a hypnotic state, tell yourself: "My subconscious mind is now totally open and receptive to everything I am saying. It will carry out all of my instructions because this is what I consciously desire." At this point you should begin giving yourself direct, positive suggestions for whatever you wish. Appendix B (see page 209) includes a sample induction talk you can use as a guide for constructing suggestions to stop smoking, lose weight, gain self-confidence, or whatever it is that you want to work on through self-hypnosis.

It's a good idea to write out your suggestions in advance so that they are exact. You must be very careful not to program your subconscious mind with incorrect suggestions. A beginner should always carefully edit his or her ideas and follow the rules outlined in the chapter on visualization (see page 145). Suggestions can be abbreviated into a key word, such as "healthy," "slender," or "confident" when you are in a hurry and don't have sufficient time for the entire program. Or, you can condense the idea into one sentence, such as: "I am now rapidly losing weight."

Repetition is the main rule in giving effective suggestions. Repeat your suggestions at least three times to be sure they penetrate your subconscious mind. Certainly, advertisers are aware of this principle; television commercials are repeated over and over again so that the conscious mind becomes bored with them and ceases to pay attention. At that point the commercial goes directly into the subconscious without hindrance.

Mental imagery should be added to your positive suggestions, because the subconscious thinks in pictures. The visualization technique is discussed fully in chapter 5 (see page 67). Suffice to say that you should, in your mind's eye, see yourself being slender, acting confidently, passing an exam, or whatever you are working on. The visual image should always represent the desired result. It's best to work on no more than two suggestions at one time so that your energy doesn't become scattered over too wide a field. Or, you can work on one objective for a week and then switch to another while your subconscious mind begins carrying out the first suggestions.

When you are ready to awaken from your hypnotic state, say to yourself: "I will easily be able to carry out all the suggestions I have given myself. The next time I do this, I will be able to go even deeper, very quickly. I will now count from one to five (or whatever your prearranged awakening signal is). At the count of five, I will awaken, completely refreshed and rejuvenated, full of energy, and feeling wonderful in every way!"

Theory of Hypnosis

Ideas are conceived in the conscious part of the mind, which turns them over to the subconscious. The subconscious responds to the idea and begins carrying it out. The conscious mind produces the *impression,* while the subconscious produces the *expression.* It is always the conscious mind that determines what is to be done, and the subconscious furnishes the power with which to do it. You, the soul, have the ability to think the thought, to make the decision, to create an idea, but you do not have the power to carry it out.

For example, if you wish to raise your hand to ask a question in class, you can consciously make the decision, but you don't know how to move the muscles involved in that act. The subconscious does the work, and you know nothing about how it operates, all you can consciously do is originate the idea.

Under hypnosis, the conscious mind relinquishes its originative ability for the time being, and turns that over to the hypnotist.

The hypnotist then temporarily becomes the originator for the individual, and thinks up the idea that the subject's subconscious will carry out. Thus, under hypnosis we form what may be termed a "composite personality" between two individuals, acting together as one (see Figure 6, below).

Remember that the subconscious mind can function only deductively, as explained in chapter 3 on "Reprogramming Your Mind." It has absolutely no power to reason, analyze, judge, select, negate, or disagree with any idea that is given to it. Ideas must be selected at the conscious level because, once a concept is accepted by the conscious mind, it penetrates the subconscious and remains there permanently, regardless of whether it is true or false, right or wrong. The simple secret of lodging an idea into the subconscious is this: *If it's logical, it lodges; and if it lodges, you're hooked!* Now, logical does not necessarily mean *true.* It simply means that the idea cannot be refuted by the present knowledge of the conscious part of the mind, and thus it is accepted, sinks into the subconscious, and becomes a part of the person's psychic fabric.

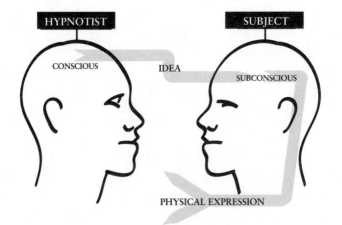

Figure 6. Composite Personality of Hypnosis.

Since the subconscious cannot reject or negate ideas given to it by the conscious mind, if you keep telling your subconscious that this or that is harmful to you, and may cause you to eventually have a heart attack, or develop cancer, or whatever destructive idea you give it, it will eventually begin carrying out your order. If you repeatedly tell your subconscious mind that you are inadequate, fearful, incompetent, unable to succeed financially, and so forth, it will accommodate you and obey your order.

If the subconscious could reject certain ideas, and select only those for our health and growth, we would never be sick, we would never fail, and we would always be happy, healthy, competent individuals, but we would not have any free will. We would all be basically the same, because the subconscious would select only constructive, positive ideas, and reject the rest. This, however, is not the function of the subconscious mind. The soul (conscious mind) must be in charge of the personality, and it is the job of the soul to select the correct, positive, healthy ideas it wants to see manifested in our lives.

When under hypnosis, you are contacting directly your subconscious mind, and it will not argue with the ideas you give it. For example, if you should tell a person under hypnosis when the subconscious is laid bare, that she has super strength, or will not feel any pain when you put a needle in her arm, Spirit will not question it, and will carry out the suggestion. The one function of the subconscious is to express the ideas that it has been given, and it never objects nor reasons upon what is said, but willingly accepts and obeys.

Ideas that get into the subconscious can come either from other people, or they may originate in the individual's own conscious mind. The important thing to remember is that ideas or concepts are lodged in every person's subconscious and, if they are of a negative character, they will sooner or later cause trouble in the individual's physical and emotional life. The subconscious mind is the power behind the throne; it is the source of dynamic energy in a person's life. It receives the impressions of the thoughts and desires of the conscious mind, and expresses them inevitably in the physical organism, and in the character and life of the person. The subconscious is the great inner world from which all things proceed. What is programmed *there* is what governs our lives!

Dr. Thurman Fleet, founder of Concept-Therapy says: "To an extent greater than you have ever dreamed, you get from life exactly what you expect innately. Your subconscious power arranges your affairs and draws to you exactly those things and conditions that you have thought about and visualized in your conscious thinking. What you are now, your position in life, is the result of past thought. There is no such thing as chance. You have visualized a certain mode of life and thought about it to such an extent that you have directed your subconscious power to manifest it for you." Thus, if you want to know what you've been asking for, look at what you've got. If you don't like it, you have the power to change it, by the very same process through which it originally became manifest.

Remember, the great Creative Power Within does not think. It has no power to reason. It cannot of itself act, but must be set in motion either from your own thought or from an impression gained from others. The techniques for transformation presented here show how you may consciously direct Spirit properly, so you can change your whole life for the better. Not only can you change your environment or your financial condition, you can even alter the state of your physical and mental health.

Remember always that the subconscious is your servant. You are the originator of ideas, and all that is required is for you to conceive positive ideas instead of negative ones. By holding these concepts in your mind constantly, they will gradually sink down into your subconscious, and then will manifest in your life. You become a creator in your own right, and create positive thoughts that, in time, will be brought into being.

So far as we know this Creative Power Within is limitless. What you really desire and confidently expect, you will receive. Therefore, use this power intelligently. Think positive, constructive thoughts, and never entertain negative, destructive ideas. If you desire something in your life that is constructive and proper for you to have, then visualize it, and you will find in time it will come to you. Repeat daily the mental picture or the suggestion and, if this is persisted in without entertaining doubts, that something will surely come to you. Your only limitations are your own thoughts—you have no other limitations!

To summarize the main points in this chapter:

1. Write out your suggestions so that they are accurate and exact.

2. Symbolize the suggestions with a key word (conditioned response).

3. Read your suggestions aloud before hypnotizing yourself, to set them in your mind.

4. Select a quiet place where you can spend an uninterrupted fifteen to thirty minutes each day practicing self-hypnosis.

5. Seat yourself in a comfortable chair with your hands resting in your lap and your legs uncrossed.

6. Fix your eyes on a spot above eye level. As you are staring at this spot, relax your body and tell yourself repeatedly that your eyelids are getting very, very heavy, and that they will soon close and stay closed until you are ready to come out of the hypnotic state.

7. With your eyes closed, talk to yourself about becoming more relaxed. Start at the top of your head and relax every muscle down to your feet, or work in a reverse pattern. Begin with your key phrase, "relax now."

8. Visualize a restful scene, such as lying down on the soft grass in the woods, taking a hot bath, going down

in an elevator to the tenth floor, and stretching out in a comfortable bed.

9. Give yourself a triggering cue, such as raising your index finger to indicate to yourself that you are now in hypnosis. When this occurs, say to yourself, "I am now in deep hypnosis."

10. Visualize the outcome of your suggestion, using as much sensory input as possible. For example, visualize yourself at your desired weight and wearing clothes that will fit you at that size. Visualize other people telling you how good you look.

11. Give yourself direct, positive suggestions that you are now doing what you want to do and being what you want to become.

12. Work on only one, or at most two, suggestions within one session.

13. Before giving the signal to awaken, tell yourself that you will carry out all the suggestions you have made and that you will go even deeper into hypnosis the next time. Remind yourself that you will feel refreshed, rejuvenated, and energetic upon awakening.

14. Practice the art of self-hypnosis every day to become an adept practitioner.

This method of self-hypnosis, if applied diligently, will help you to achieve your desired goals in life. Excellent progress in self-development can be made by anyone who is willing to take the time to form a relationship with his or her subconscious mind. You have the power; all you need to do is apply it!

Hypnosis is the key to a happier life and the means whereby we can contact our higher self. This Great Power within us stands ready to serve our every need, if only we will call upon it. By means of this technique, you can set your goals and reach them, and learn how to gain information from your subconscious mind you are not consciously aware of. In ancient Greece there was an inscription over the Temple of Delphos that simply stated: "Know Thyself." Hypnosis is a means whereby one can come into contact with the deepest part of oneself, and thereby live a much fuller life.

Imagination is the beginning of creation.
You imagine what you desire, you will what you
imagine and at last you create what you will.

GEORGE BERNARD SHAW

FIVE

Imagination: Your Key to the Kingdom

All of the world's great men and women have used the power of imagination to create their successful lives. They have become great because they dared to imagine grand achievements. They constantly pictured in their minds what they wanted, and the Creative Power Within, given these pictures to work on, eventually brought them into being. Whatever is occurring now in your life is the result of an image in your mind, and whatever will happen in the future will be the result of *your* images, not someone else's. This requires you to make a correct image of what you want to see happen in your life or personality, and turn that image over to the Creative Power Within to manifest it. We are all directly or indirectly responsible for almost everything

that happens to us, even though it's often easier to blame someone or something else. Of course there are some circumstances
beyond our control, such as natural disasters, etc. But, if we have
knowledge of how the mind works, we will recognize that the
way we think and feel has an intimate connection with what is
happening to us.

If we get up in the morning thinking it's going to be a bad day
with nothing going right, that's probably what will occur. Our
thoughts go out into the universe in the form of vibrations and
attract to us exactly what we are sending out. If you are always
surrounded by difficulties, the solution is to change the picture
in your mind and image a more positive, fulfilling life.

Creative visualization is the technique of using your imagination in a systematic, structured way to create what you want. Of
course, we all use our imagination constantly, usually in an
unconscious, haphazard, or negative fashion. Worry, for example, is an extremely powerful image, and worried thoughts are
always negative and destructive. Every time you fret about not
getting the raise you want, possibly getting laid-off, having a car
accident, or not making your sales quota, you are programming
your mind destructively. Since we have been taught so many negative concepts about ourselves, we automatically expect and
imagine that we will have difficulties, limitations, and misfor-
tunes, thus bringing it into being.

Properly directed, imagination is the key to the doorway to
success, love, health, abundance, satisfying relationships, self-confidence, and greater self-expression. All we need to do is become
consciously aware of what we are creating, and change the programming if we don't like it.

Everyone has a basic concept about themselves, formed
mainly by the ideas others gave us in early life, and also by the
feedback we receive from people in our everyday lives. Unfortunately, many people's basic concept of themselves includes ideas
such as failure, rejection, inferiority, ill health, worthlessness,

financial instability, and other destructive thoughts. Let's analyze the type of suggestions many people have been given during the process of growing up. Some typical basic concepts I frequently hear from my clients are:

"I'm not capable of earning a good living."

"I feel inferior to many people."

"I'm too sensitive, everything upsets me."

"I can't get good grades in school."

"I have a poor memory."

"I'll never be successful."

"I'm not as smart as other people."

"I can't get organized."

"I think I'm not very lovable."

All of us have been exposed to negative ideas like these as we grew up. Do you remember your parents saying things like, "you'll never amount to anything," "you can't do anything right," "you're really stupid," "you're so awkward and clumsy," "you're really not very bright," "you're lazy and selfish," "you're the pretty one, but Marsha's the intelligent one," or similar phrases? Or, maybe a teacher told you, "you can't spell so you might as well forget it," "you'll never be able to do math," or "you just have a rotten memory." Statements such as these, though often intended to motivate, acutely impair our confidence and self-esteem. Constant reinforcement of such negative ideas may cause us to feel socially inadequate and unable to communicate with others.

Some time ago I facilitated a therapy group in which a woman stated that her mother constantly told her: "Oh Mary, you just don't have any personality." And she didn't. This unfortunate woman was inhibited from developing her social skills, and her natural self-expression was thwarted by the dominant idea she was inadequate. If you feel this way, your self-concept is the cause of it all. We place our own limitations upon ourselves, and it's nothing more than an idea operating in the subconscious mind. Granted, many of these negative ideas were given to us by others when we were too young and too helpless to reject them. But now that we are adults, we can change them and reprogram our minds by the same process.

Your future is determined by the thoughts you think today. What you think you are—*you are!* You can become whatever you would like to be. In his wonderful book *The Crack in the Cosmic Egg,* Joseph Chilton Pearce talks about the "statistical world," the so-called world of reality. Many people are fond of stating that they are "realistic," thus, they lock themselves into the statistical world, invariably bowing before the dictates of statistics and "facts," and believe that what happens to them is just the result of random chance.

We are constantly being programmed to statistics, such as "So many people in this room will die of cancer this year," "Five hundred people will be killed on our highways this holiday weekend," "Jobs these days are hard to get because many companies are still laying off people." Of course these may be facts. The statistical world is a reality because there are people who will make those statistics come true. They are people who have little control over their lives because they know nothing about the power of their own minds, and they are the helpless victims of life's vicissitudes. One who is able to think positively, however, and control his or her thoughts, need not be caught in the trap of statistics. Such a person can consciously be superior to the "Slings and arrows of outrageous fortune." As Pearce states, "An ultimately serious commitment of mind, combined with the active use of imagination, can be the determining factor in any issue, overcoming all the odds against you, and overcoming chance."

In making images for the things you desire, you must be careful not to discuss them with people who cannot share your vision. A negative person can totally destroy your image by causing you to doubt its credibility. Holding an image of your desire takes a great deal of energy, especially when the odds may be against your achieving it. You have to work hard enough at overcoming your own doubt without allowing others, who do not understand the power of the mind, to influence you. Pearce states that *"nonambiguity is the shaping force of reality!"* This is a tremendously important statement. It means that when you remove all doubt that you will receive what you have imaged, it is sure to come to you. Believe in your images with all your strength, and don't allow nonbelievers to distort or destroy your faith by quoting statistics, or telling you all the reasons you cannot achieve them.

Creativity and Imagination

Creating what you want in life depends upon the use of the most potent force in the world: imagination. *By sustaining mental images of any kind—good or bad—you will eventually bring about a physical effect,* provided only that your images are logical. Unfortunately, our educational system stifles imagination by placing all the emphasis on rational thought. That's one reason our young people are so bored with school. If you have a child with an active imagination, you have a potential genius, because all creative people have highly developed imaginations. That is the source of their ideas, the realm of the inner life. Einstein stated: "Imagination is more important than knowledge," adding that many of his ideas came to him while he was daydreaming or fantasizing, and not while he was applying his intellect to a problem.

Since creativity—the ability to look at things in a different and original way—depends upon imagination, it follows that if we wish to be more creative, we can do so by developing our imagination. Artists, writers, and musicians appear to be born with a great imaginative ability, but this skill can be learned by anyone. Sometimes in my seminars people will tell me that they cannot visualize any of the things I suggest during the process. This is not really so; everyone can visualize things, but we all do this differently. Some people actually visualize an image projected before them when they close their eyes, but others merely "get a feeling" of the object, activity, or event. If you could not visualize things you would never find your way home, because you have a picture in your mind of what your house looks like, and what streets you need to take to find it. If you didn't hold an image in your mind of the people in your environment, you wouldn't recognize them the next time you saw them. Your mental picture matches the way they appear to you, and you could draw a picture of your loved ones, no matter how crudely, if you were required to do so.

Visualization and Psychotherapy

One of the early pioneers of visualization, Dr. Joseph Wolpe, a psychiatrist at the University of Virginia School of Medicine, used imagery as a way to help people suffering from phobias. He believed that a phobia was a learned behavior, not a result of childhood trauma, and that the phobia could be "unlearned" if his patient could develop an opposite response to fear. He hit on the idea of teaching phobic people to relax deeply in the presence of the desired object; after all, one cannot be afraid and relaxed at the same time. There was a drawback to the procedure, however, because it was sometimes not practical to be present with his patients when they faced the thing they feared, such as flying in a plane. Dr. Wolpe then experimented with having his patients *imagine* the phobic object while relaxed. It worked. In a few short sessions, his patients were able to overcome phobias they'd had for years through this method, which psychologists call "systematic desensitization." Imagery is now widely used in modern psychotherapy and has proven to be extremely effective in helping clients handle life crises.

Barbara, a homemaker who had become so depressed she had great difficulty getting up in the morning, came to see me for therapy a few years ago. She could barely summon the energy to dress before her husband returned home from work, and it took all the stamina she had to come to my office. In the evening she would gather all her energy to prepare a simple dinner for herself and her husband, and then would sit in front of the television, sinking further into depression. In the course of her treatment, I asked her to make a list of "reinforcing events," things she had formerly enjoyed doing, since it's very important for depressed people to schedule activities each day that they enjoy. I usually ask the client to incorporate at least one of these activities into his or her daily regimen. But this woman was too depressed even to attempt small pleasures such as taking a walk in the park, getting her hair styled, or meeting a friend for coffee. Stymied, I asked her to spend some time each day mentally rehearsing the activities on her list. In a short time she was able to translate the fantasies into reality, and her life became more enjoyable.

There are many uses for structured visualization. Another client of mine, a young law student, was scheduled to take the bar examination in a few months, and she was terrified of failing. After years of hard study to acquire her law degree, Marilyn felt her entire future hung in the balance, and she would be devastated if she were to fail the exam and not get admitted to the bar. For several weeks I worked with her on visualizing herself being calm and relaxed while taking the exam, with her mind clear and alert, and the answers flashing to her readily. We also developed an image of the future in which she went to the local newspaper office and saw her name posted on the bulletin board, listed among those who had successfully passed. Additionally, she saw herself receiving the official notice in the mail, and imaged her family congratulating her on her success. Happily, her image came true; she passed in the top quarter.

Visualization and Sports

Many coaches today use the transformational technique of visualization as a significant part of their athletes' training regimen. Charles Garfield, a former weightlifter and psychologist at the University of California in Berkeley, reported in *Brain/Mind Bulletin* (March 1980), that he had used visualization with Olympic hopefuls to optimize their athletic performance. "The key," Garfield stated, "is to visualize with the clarity necessary to really feel yourself in the situation. The central nervous system doesn't know the difference between deep, powerful visualization and the event itself, so the physical followup of the actual event is merely an after-the-fact duplication of an event already performed and completed in imagery."

Visualization worked superbly for Chris Evert, now retired, who was a top-seeded professional tennis player. Before every match she sat down, relaxed, and visualized her every move, seeing herself return every one of her opponent's volleys and eventually winning the match. Her impressive record validates the effectiveness of this approach.

Mike Spino, director of the Esalen Sports Center in Big Sur, California, coaches long-distance runners by using visualization. The runners image a big hand at their backs giving assistance during the race and providing something to lean into when fatigued. Spino believes that visualization techniques will be among the most important aspects of athletic training in the future. Edmond Jacobson, a psychologist famous for his relaxation technique, has demonstrated that if a person imagines himself running, small but measurable amounts of contraction actually take place in the muscles used for running.*

---

* Jacobson, Edmund. *Progressive Relaxation,* University of Chicago Press, 1974.

The Center for Accelerated Learning in Wisconsin conducted a study with students from four universities that proved that imagery improves learning and recall. According to the federally funded research, college students using mental imagery performed 12 percent better on immediate recall than students learning the same material without mental imagery. Furthermore, those using the imagery performed 26 percent better on long-term retention than those not using it.†

The Mind/Body Connection

Imagery works because *the subconscious cannot tell the difference between something that is strongly imagined and something that is actually taking place in the physical world.* Anatomists have proven there are pathways between the part of the brain where we store our pictures, and the autonomic nervous system that controls involuntary activities such as breathing, heart rate, and blood pressure. There are also pathways from the autonomic nervous system to the glands, such as the pituitary and adrenals. This means that a picture in our minds has an impact on every cell in our bodies. Thinking is not only an action of the mind, but an action of the entire body.

In his book *The Body of Life,* Thomas Hanna writes:

> The nature of our thinking activity automatically determines the nature of our bodily activity. . . . When we think the same thoughts of revenge over and over again, we are activating the muscles and glands of our bodies over and over again. When we repeat the same thoughts of disappointment over and over we are repeatedly stamping their motor power into the tissues of our body until they sag in forlornness.

Understanding this intimate connection between mind and body, we can rejuvenate ourselves physically and mentally through

---

† Meier. Center for Accelerated Learning, 1103 Wisconsin St., Lake Geneva, Wisc. 53147.

positive images. The greatest proof of this is demonstrated by hypnosis. In my self-hypnosis seminars, I have been privileged to witness the remarkable powers of the subconscious mind. On several occasions I have demonstrated the amazing control of the mind over the body by simple experiments such as painlessly inserting a hat pin a half-inch deep into the flesh of a subject's arm. When the hat pin is removed, there is no pain, no blood, and no aftereffect. The puncture hole is completely gone within a few moments, and often the subject is not even aware that the needle was placed into his or her arm.

The subconscious is God-like; it is all-knowing and all-healing, and it will take care of you if you give it a chance. It never sleeps; if it did, you would not wake up in the morning because your subconscious takes care of your breathing, the circulation of your blood, your digestion, and every other bodily function while your conscious mind sleeps.

All you have to do is repeatedly tell your subconscious what you want, and it will then set about producing it. Unfortunately, instead of working positively to achieve what they want, many people start worrying about not getting it. This sends out negative energy, and you end up holding a picture in your mind that you won't obtain the desired result. You can add more negative energy to that by telling your friends you wish you could have this or that, but probably won't be able to. Then they, in turn, also hold the negative image. In this way you keep constantly giving a message to your subconscious mind *not* to bring you what you desire. The subconscious is a fertile field; whatever you plant is what you will reap.

How to Visualize Creatively

The art of visualization is a transformation technique you can use to obtain anything you want in life: love, prosperity, self-confidence, weight loss, a new job or car—whatever you wish. Imaging is a very precise methodology that can transform your life, but there are certain rules governing it. Here, then, are the steps to follow to create your own reality through creative visualization.

First, find a quiet place where you will be totally undisturbed and can completely relax. As studies in hypnosis demonstrate, the subconscious mind is very suggestible when we are in a relaxed state; thus the more deeply you can relax, the more effective your visualization. If you are not accustomed to deep relaxation, refer to Appendix A, or use the technique described in the chapter on self-hypnosis (see page 56). Of course, never try to visualize when the radio or television is on, or when the kids are running through the house. If you can find no other place where you can be undisturbed for at least ten minutes, lock yourself in the bathroom.

1. Phrase It Positively

Before beginning your imagery, make up a short, concise summary of exactly what you want, and always put it in the positive. For example, if you are working on weight loss, never say, "I will not be fat." This vibrates the cells in your brain connected with the image of obesity and reinforces the idea that you are overweight. Even though this may be true, don't strengthen the image by reminding yourself. Say, rather, "I am always going to be slim," or "I am becoming slimmer every day." If you feel inadequate, don't say, "I am overcoming my inferiority complex," and thus convince your subconscious that you have one, which will increase your anxiety. Instead, say: "I am becoming more confident every day."

A good friend of mine, who is overweight, invited me to her home for dinner one evening. When I arrived I found a picture of a huge hippopotamus pasted on her refrigerator door. "Ella," I said, "look what you're doing to yourself. You're telling your subconscious mind that you think you look like a fat hippo, and you're driving in the idea that you're overweight every time you walk by that picture." I suggested she clip a picture of a slender model from a fashion catalog, paste a photo of her own face over the model's, and attach that to the refrigerator. "Let your subconscious know what you want," I suggested, "not what you don't want!"

Statements about your image should never be placed in the future, as, for example: "Soon I will be slender," or "I will get a job." Sure you will, but it may be another year if you phrase it so vaguely. Some practitioners of visualization believe that you should express your affirmations as though you already have what you want. I disagree, for that violates the next principle, which is that images must be logical to reach the subconscious mind. It is not logical to say "I am now slender," if you currently weigh two hundred pounds. I suggest using the phrase, "I am becoming. . ." "Every day I am becoming more slender," or "I am becoming more confident every day."

In dealing with specific things you desire, you can name a time limit: "By this spring I will have my new car." "I am now losing two pounds a week, and by Christmas I will weigh 120 pounds." "I will start my new job by the first of March."

Your positive statements can be written on 3 x 5 cards and placed by your bedside, on the bathroom mirror, or on the dashboard of your car—any place where you can see them frequently and repeat them, thus giving your subconscious mind ample reminders throughout the day. I like to put my imagery cards next to the alarm clock on my nightstand so that they are the last thing I see at night and the first thing I see in the morning. If you can visualize your desire at bedtime and fall asleep holding that thought, your subconscious will be able to work on it all night long, without any interference, and the process will be more effective.

2. Make It Logical

The key to getting a message into the subconscious mind is: *If it's logical, it lodges; and if it lodges, you're hooked!* Remember, logical doesn't necessarily mean true. If, when you were six years old, you were told by mom or dad that you were awkward, clumsy, and not as bright as your sister, that suggestion would probably have been logical to you. After all, a parent is like a god to a child, so surely they knew what kind of person you were. Our personalities are formed by what we are told about ourselves in the process of growing up, even if it wasn't true. If something is said to you that appears to be logical and you have no way to refute it, it becomes accepted by your subconscious and becomes a part of you.

On the other hand, if a statement is not logical to you, the conscious mind will simply not accept it, or will refute it, and it doesn't get past the psychic barrier into the subconscious. Thus, if your conscious mind cannot fully believe your image, it will not be accepted by your subconscious. For instance, if you wish to make some money, you should not say: "I'm going to earn a million dollars by the end of the year." For most of us this is completely illogical, so the subconscious will not accept it. If you want to lose weight, you shouldn't say: "I'll lose thirty pounds by the end of the month," because you probably won't be able to convince yourself you can.

3. Be Specific

The more detail you can bring into your image, the easier it will be for your subconscious to carry it out. The subconscious mind is quite literal, and it needs to be given accurate directions. Of course, this is not always possible, but whenever it is, take the time to think out each detail of your image. If you are looking for a new job, you may not be able to specify the particular building you would like to work in, but you can image yourself smiling and happy as you walk around your new office.

For example, if you would like to move to a new house, think out in advance all the things that you want to have in your home. Would you like a garden or a small yard that needs little care? Do you want a two-car garage, lots of storage space, a large kitchen, three bedrooms, two baths, a fireplace, and a swimming pool? Be specific, but here again, make it logical. Don't ask for a house that is obviously beyond your means, thus making it illogical for you to obtain it.

Years ago when I lived in San Francisco, I planned to move to San Jose to begin my postgraduate studies. I knew little about the city, having only driven through it a couple of times. I didn't have any friends there, so I had no one to advise me on a good location in which to live. But, instead of just driving around aimlessly in my car looking for an apartment, I sat down one morning and typed the following:

> I am going to San Jose today to find an apartment that—
>
> —is quiet so that I can study undisturbed.
>
> —is close to the university.
>
> —is in a good neighborhood where I will feel safe.
>
> —is spacious and clean.
>
> —is bright and cheery and has lots of windows.
>
> —allows pets.
>
> —is in a price range of $____ to $____.

I closed my eyes for a few minutes and imagined myself walking around in my new apartment feeling happy and content. Then I turned my image over to the Creative Power Within, knowing that it knew the area much better than I did and could lead me to the place I desired. By evening I had put down a deposit on an apartment that met my specifications exactly, except that the price was somewhat higher than I had wished because my range hadn't been logical!

In the past when I had moved, I searched for weeks for places to live by trying to do it solely on my own without asking for help from the great powerhouse of knowledge within. But I had now learned that the method of directing and ordering my life by working with Spirit in a harmonious partnership is so much easier than doing things with my limited conscious mind. If you can learn to do everything in cooperation with the Creative Power Within, your life can be so much simpler.

At this point we must caution about dealing with cosmic laws. Using mind-power and imagery means calling upon all the forces of the universe to attain what we want. These forces are extremely powerful and can create problems if used for wrong action, for this invariably brings suffering to the user. Those who use their mind-power to bring harm or adversity to another will find that misfortune eventually comes to them. There is really only *one life* and anything we do to others eventually comes back to us. We are all familiar with "black magic," which has been used for centuries to hurt others through mental powers. We might say that positive visualization is "white magic," and it works on the same principle. When using creative imagery therefore, heed this cosmic law: *Never manipulate the will of another!* If you do, it will boomerang on you and cause serious trouble in your life.

For example, if you want a new house, you can certainly visualize one similar to an admired house of neighbors or friends, but never visualize specifically for their house. If you want money, never use imagery that a specific person will give it to you. Simply imagine it coming to you: receiving a check in the mail, putting a deposit in the bank, buying something that you want with the money. Leave it up to Spirit to select the means whereby the money will come; you don't need to concern yourself with that.

Ron, a salesperson, attended my seminar on imagery and immediately went home to image a potential customer signing a contract with him the next day. Ron relaxed in a living room chair and visualized himself driving to the customer's house, greeting the man as he opened the door, making his sales presentation, and seeing the man sign a contract for a very large deal.

This is a direct violation of cosmic law, for Ron was deliberately manipulating his customer's will. But, what is the difference between a salesperson's trying to persuade a customer to buy, and visualizing him making that purchase? The difference is that persuasion is done at a conscious level. We try to persuade people to do what we want every day of our lives, and there's nothing wrong with that, simply because people know what we are attempting to do and they can consciously resist it and defend against it if they want. On the other hand, when you visualize someone carrying out your desire, they are defenseless. They are your helpless victim and, without any conscious knowledge of why they are doing it, can easily fall under the power of your concentrated thought. In short, it isn't fair.

What Ron should have done in this case was visualize himself reaching a certain sales goal that month, telling his wife he had increased his commissions, winning the company award for topping the sales quota, depositing money in the bank, or even buying things he wanted with the extra cash. This would not have involved directly manipulating the will of another, but would leave it up to Spirit to provide the means whereby he achieved his desire.

A few years ago the tabloids reported the story of a man who saw a woman every morning on the elevator in his apartment building as he went to work. He found the woman attractive and, although he had never spoken to her, decided he was going to marry her. Obviously, he was not interested in her qualities as a person, merely in her physical appearance. Since he had taken a course in mind control, he decided to visualize himself walking up the aisle with the woman and being married by his minister. The next morning he introduced himself to her and began a courtship, all the while imaging, without her knowledge, that he would marry her. Sure enough, within three months, his proposal and engagement ring were accepted and they were married. This marriage will probably come to a disastrous end because this man deliberately manipulated the woman's unconscious mind and violated the cosmic law of *noninterference with the will of another.* Such misuse of mind powers can create great havoc in an individual's life and in the lives of his or her unknowing victims. It is tantamount to a criminal act to take advantage of people without their consent.

This certainly doesn't mean that you can't visualize a happy marriage. If you want to get married or be in a relationship, imaging for that is not only appropriate but desirable; just be careful not to image for a particular person. If you want to be in a relationship, the sensible action to take would be to make a list of the qualities you desire in a partner. This is something people seldom think of, and often they don't even know what qualities would be most compatible with their own personality. Sometimes people get married because they both like dancing or old movies, or some other inconsequential reason that doesn't mean much after the initial glow of romance has dimmed. The more similarities people have, the more likely it is they will have a harmonious relationship. The more dissimilarity, the greater the potential problems because every difference can be a point of conflict.

Although it is a violation of cosmic law to use imagery for a specific person, you can imagine yourself being in a relationship and doing things with a loving partner. You can feel your happiness at being with a person who really loves you, and you can imagine coming home after work and being greeted affectionately by such a person. If you wish to be married, it's perfectly fine to imagine yourself in a wedding setting and feel the happiness you expect to experience at that event, provided you don't imagine a particular person as your mate.

But, what if you've already met someone to whom you feel tremendously attracted? Let's say it's a man at the office. Though you must not specifically image him asking you out on a date or walking up the aisle with you, you are certainly free to send him all the positive, loving thoughts you want. There is nothing wrong with thinking loving thoughts because you are not manipulating someone by doing that, as long as you don't visualize him actually doing something with you. But you can be sure that he will pick this up, at least on the subconscious level, and will begin to respond warmly to you. You can visualize him surrounded by a lovely, soft, warm cloud of pink (the color of love) and see that color flowing from you to him. You can do the same thing if you're already in a relationship and want to create a harmonious feeling between you and your partner. You'll be amazed at the results!

Some years ago I taught Concept-Therapy classes in the Bay area with another instructor, Dr. Charles Craig. Mr. and Mrs. K came to every one of our classes and usually sat in the front row. One day, one of the students mentioned to me that Mrs. K had told her she enjoyed the lessons, but didn't care for the way I presented them. Mrs. K couldn't seem to identify specifically what it was about my presentation that bothered her, but I strongly suspected it was Mr. K's intense interest in the classes, and his habit of coming over and discussing the material with me at every coffee break.

Realizing the importance of maintaining a harmonious relationship with all the students, and knowing my teaching would be disrupted if anyone were sending me negative vibrations, I thought it wise to rectify the situation. I liked Mrs. K and had no adverse feelings toward her, and certainly wasn't interested in her husband, so it was easy for me to mentally send her positive, loving thoughts. I found a class photograph with her picture in it, put it on my bureau, and began talking to the photo, telling Mrs. K that I liked and respected her and that she had no reason to feel threatened by me. I would say positive things like this aloud every time I walked by the picture.

At our next class, two weeks later, Mrs. K brought a beautiful flower arrangement for the podium, which she handed to me, and she sat beaming throughout the class. Later she told Dr. Craig that she had been feeling very positive about my presentation and realized I was really a good instructor. Transformation had occurred merely from thinking positively, without any direct attempt to manipulate her will or get her to do something!

4. Take Enough Time

How long will it take to manifest your image? This is a variable that depends on your ability to concentrate and visualize, and also on the severity of the problem. Naturally, if you are trying to change lifelong feelings of inferiority, it will take some time; five minutes of visualization won't erase thirty years of negative thinking.

It has been established that it takes at least thirty-three seconds, as a bare minimum, for a suggestion to reach the subconscious mind. That's why television commercials are usually at least that long. Also, psychologists have determined that, on the average, it takes about twenty-one days to change a habit. The same principle applies to images. But, as your ability to visualize becomes perfected through repetition, you will find that many of your images will manifest sooner. Some people have reached a point where, through continued practice, some of their images come true within a few days, or even hours. How often should you visualize? A good goal to set is two or three times a day for ten to fifteen minutes per session. The more you practice and develop your power of visualization, the faster your images will come true.

Feeling and emotion profoundly affect the amount of time it takes to get an idea into the subconscious mind. When something is said to you that has an intense emotional impact, it slams into the subconscious the instant you hear it. If, for example, a parent or teacher or boss says, "you're really stupid," that thought immediately penetrates your subconscious mind. Unfortunately, when you begin working on changing a powerful suggestion like that, the same emotion is not behind it that was there when you originally heard it, so it takes longer to change, and requires repetition of the opposite concept.

5. Get the Feeling

An important aspect of an image is the emotion behind it. The more feeling you can get into your visualization, the more convinced your subconscious will be that this is actually happening to you. *Act as if* you actually have the thing you desire and let your body experience the feelings you would have if you did. For example, if you wish to lose weight, *get the feeling* of how happy you will be wearing clothes that were formerly too tight for you, hearing people congratulate you on your weight loss, looking at yourself in the mirror and feeling very proud of yourself.

If you want a new car, imagine how good you will feel driving it down the freeway or pulling up in front of a friend's house in it. *Remember, the subconscious can't tell the difference between something that is vividly imagined and something that is happening in reality,* so very soon it will make it a reality for you, provided, of course, that it's logical. The more capable you are of living in the feeling of the dream fulfilled, the greater your capacity to actually receive your desire.

6. Take Some Action on the Physical Plane

You must impress your subconscious that you mean business. If, for example, you are working on weight loss, cut down on your food intake. If you're eating like a horse, you can visualize all day, and nothing will happen, because your subconscious is getting a double message. If you wish to get a new job, begin looking at the classified ads, sending out résumés, and networking with well-placed friends. If you want to be in a relationship, go out to places where there is an opportunity to meet the type of person you want.

One evening I visited with Doris, a young student of mine, and found her living room full of boxes containing most of her belongings. Doris was working her way through college and could only afford to live in an apartment building filled with other students whose stereos blared day and night. She told me she could no longer put up with the noise and she was planning to move to a quieter building and get a room by herself. I asked how that was possible on her limited income.

"Well," she replied with a slight smugness, "I learned in your class that if you want something to happen in your life, you first make an image, so I've been visualizing a new apartment every day. I decided packing up everything I don't immediately need would be taking action to convince my subconscious mind that I'm serious, so that it will help me find a better place to live. Even if I have to stay here a few more months, I'm *acting as if* I'm moving, and that makes me feel better!"

Indeed, her subconscious got her message and did carry out her image shortly thereafter. Within a few weeks of my visit, Doris found an apartment a few blocks from the college at only slightly more rent than she had been paying.

The Effect of Concentration

In order for an image to manifest, you must *concentrate* on it, and that is a protection. It means that any little fleeting thought we have will not automatically manifest in our lives—fortunately! If they did, we'd all be sorry for many of the things we created for ourselves and others through careless thinking. When something doesn't happen on schedule, our tendency is to indulge in negative thinking. For instance, if our partner doesn't arrive home at the usual time, often our first reaction is to begin worrying that he or she has been in an accident. Most of the time, we tend to think the worst, not the best. This sends out negative energy to the individual, and although it doesn't actually create the situation, it certainly doesn't help things. The best action under such circumstances is to sit down and take a few moments to visualize the person completely surrounded by a beautiful white light protecting them from any adverse forces. This is an ancient metaphysical method of psychic protection used for centuries to insulate a person from negative thoughts and forces. Then, visualize your loved one smiling, perfectly safe, coming in the front door.

Strong concentration is necessary to manifest an image, and the greater your ability to concentrate, the sooner your images will manifest for you. Concentration is an ability that can be developed; it is a learned skill just like any other. Training your mind day after day to focus on a particular image is a good way to develop your ability to concentrate.

In summary, here are the steps for creating your own reality through imagery:

1. Phrase it positively.

2. Make it logical.

3. Be specific.

4. Take enough time.

5. Visualize the *end result*.

6. Get the *feeling* that you already have your desire.

7. Take some action on the physical plane.

8. Never manipulate the will of another.

9. Repetition and concentration will manifest your desire.

Imagination is the key to all creativity and to all changes in your life and personality! It's not faith that makes all things possible, it's imagination. If you can imagine it, you can have it, provided only that it's logical. By sustaining mental images of any kind (good or bad), you will eventually bring about their manifestation in the physical world. You *are* what you imagine yourself to be! Whether you think you can, or you think you can't, you're always right. As Richard Bach wrote in *Illusions:* "Argue for your limitations, and you get to keep them."

Dreams are the seedlings of realities. Your circumstances may be uncongenial but they shall not long remain so if you but perceive an ideal and strive to reach it.

JAMES ALLEN, *As a Man Thinketh*

SIX
How to Achieve Prosperity Consciousness

Most people believe that wealth is the result of years of hard work and careful saving, unless one has inherited a fortune. This is a delusion. Statistics indicate that the majority of people in the United States, after spending the major part of their lives in work they sometimes didn't even enjoy, end up barely able to survive on social security and a small pension, if they have one at all. Reprogramming your ideas about money will attract it to you far more quickly than working a twelve-hour day and diligently saving every nickel. The road to riches is paved with strong, positive ideas, held constantly in the mind, eventually attracting an abundance of money into your life. Accumulating wealth is the result of an attitude, and not the outcome of hard labor; thus, changing your attitude is the key to becoming rich. Your inner feeling about money determines whether or not you will have it, because that to which you give your attention is what manifests in your life. If you focus attention on the lack of money and the fear of poverty, that is what's reinforced and becomes a reality for you. All human wealth is created by the human mind, and those who believe they deserve to be wealthy can create it.

A common myth about money is that there isn't enough of it for everybody. This is ridiculous because there are billions of dollars in the United States Treasury, and you deserve your fair share. Don't fall into the negative attitude of resenting affluent people, those who may have amassed far more than their share. If you resent wealthy people, you'll end up resenting yourself when you make money. Focus on the positive; you will be contributing to raising the consciousness of others by serving as an example, and you can say: "Look at me, I wasn't born rich, but I've become prosperous by changing my thinking, and you can do it too." Remember, the money you make goes back into the economy to be distributed to others, which helps prosper everyone you buy from or give money to.

You may think, "This is no time to make money because the cost of living is so high, it's almost impossible to save money and become wealthy." This is another myth, because there have been people who've become wealthy in every economic crisis this country has ever had. Many people make fortunes during an inflationary period, and you can be one of them. The particular state of the economy doesn't have to affect your personal situation if you learn to think positively and control your fears. Rise above the statistical world with positive thinking!

You Deserve to Be Wealthy

Before you can become rich, you must believe that you deserve it. It's impossible to convince your subconscious mind to bring you money if you have been programmed to the idea that you don't deserve it. We have all heard stories of people who had the ability to make a fortune but lacked the ability to keep it. Such people don't feel worthy of success; they don't think they deserve all that money, so they invariably sabotage themselves when they acquire it.

A man I knew in Toronto made a fortune as the owner of a camera store. When he had built his business to the point where he could retire and let his staff manage it, he suddenly began making mistakes: acquiring inventory he couldn't sell, firing his best manager, closing the store at peak hours. In a short time his business went downhill, and he went into debt. This so discouraged him that he began mismanaging his funds, and very soon he had to declare bankruptcy. He blamed his wife for the cause of his problems, divorced her, and started a picture framing business. Within a few years he was equally successful and once again wealthy. Again, he couldn't handle it. He made some under-the-counter deals on the fringe of the law, cut some corners and damaged his reputation, and eventually had to close his doors.

Sometimes it's not a fear of success but a fear of failure that prevents people from becoming wealthy. A person may be going along well, accumulating money, and then begins to worry: "I'm making money now, but how long will it last? What if I lost it all? What if people stop buying from me?" "What if the stock market crashes?" "What if I lose my job?" and so on. Although it's important to be prudent enough to provide for extenuating circumstances, such as a company layoff, we must constantly counteract these negative ideas with positive affirmations such as, "I deserve to be wealthy," "I deserve happiness," "I deserve success." As soon as you get these thoughts firmly implanted in your consciousness, you have taken a giant step toward achieving wealth.

Poverty Consciousness

Before discussing the use of affirmations to develop a prosperity consciousness, let's look at some of the negative statements you may have acquired about money, because these need to be eliminated before you can make any progress. What did your parents tell you about money? What were their attitudes? Did they tell you that you were capable of earning a million dollars if you wanted to, or did they say, "You'll never amount to a hill of beans!" Women in our society used to be told that they had no need to make money because a man would always take care of them.

An excellent beginning exercise is to write down on a piece of paper all the negative things you can remember your parents, relatives, teachers, coworkers, and close friends telling you about money. Please take a moment now before you read any further to complete this exercise. It's important to take the time to do it because it will help you discover what concepts have been programmed into your subconscious about money. Once you know them, you can set about systematically to remove them. You also may have programmed your own subconscious into many negative ideas about money, for example: "I don't deserve to make money because . . ."

— I don't have enough education.

— I'm locked into a job that doesn't pay very much, and I don't know how to do anything else.

— I married too young, and I now have too many responsibilities.

— I've gotten myself so deeply in debt that I'll never be able to get out.

— I can't be spiritual and make money too.

— I can't get a high-paying job because I'm female.

— I shouldn't make more money than my husband.

— My parents said I wasn't very bright, so I don't
deserve it.

— My parents never had much, so I don't expect much
either.

— I'm too young (*or* too old).

— I've never been able to get what I want, and I know
I won't now.

— I don't have enough skills.

If you harbor ideas like these, you will eventually become discouraged and decide that you're not going to make a lot of money. Although millions of people seek wealth and would like to have a financially secure future, they defeat themselves by this type of thinking. They have tried everything but changing their thoughts—the one thing that would make all the difference.

The power of thought is the only thing over which you have unquestionable control. A definite, strong idea, when it is held constantly in the mind, can actually change the biochemistry of the brain so that it will no longer be programmed for failure or defeat. Thoughts are things; they have an electromagnetic reality, and they create their visible counterpart in the outer world. If you change your inner thoughts, your outer conditions must also change. That is a natural law. So begin now to have constant vigilance over your thoughts. Never again allow yourself to say, "I can't afford it," rather say, "I'm going to buy it. I'm planning for it now."

For instance, if you want to visit Europe, don't defeat your plans by thinking you'll never be able to afford it. Say instead, "I'm working on my trip to Europe now," and then set about collecting pictures and articles of places you would like to visit. Get a special box to hold your collection of information. Label it *My Trip to Europe*. Each time you place an item in your box, the idea will become a little more possible, a little closer to its physical manifestation. Your thoughts will begin to draw to you the money you need to accomplish your dream, and your physical experience will follow your image.

Reverend Ike, the famous preacher who inspired thousands with his sermons on prosperity consciousness, tells about his youth in Harlem. Whenever his friends saw a white man driving a big, expensive car through the area they would grumble about the "honkies" who kept them in poverty. Instead of complaining, Reverend Ike would say, "That's my car; there goes my car. I'm going to own one just like that." And now he does—in fact, several! Instead of resenting them for their wealth, he identified with them, and became just as prosperous.

After graduating from college I worked as a therapist for a government-funded mental health agency that was very limited in its ability to pay its counselors. I earned five dollars an hour and was barely surviving. One Monday morning, a colleague, Mike, announced that he had spent the weekend in a workshop with Leonard Orr, a wealthy San Franciscan who was teaching people how to develop "prosperity consciousness." Mike said Leonard taught him how to make affirmations to attract money into his life, and he shared the method with me. Since I already knew about the power of the mind and had used visualization to change many other aspects of my life, I decided to use these ideas to increase my salary. Three weeks later, after having spent two years at the agency without a raise, my salary was increased by a few dollars. Excitedly, I told the director that my affirmations had worked. "You call that prosperity?" he replied with a smirk. "Around here it is," I retorted, but I knew that was only a beginning. I kept making my affirmations, and small things began to happen almost immediately. An unexpected check refunding an overpayment on a loan arrived in the mail. Then I received a large tax refund I had not counted on. Within a month, I was offered another job at a tremendous salary increase.

Success is a much more empowering concept than failure. Just as it takes more energy to frown than to smile, it also takes more energy to fail than to succeed because it takes a lot of concentrated energy to hold on to negative ideas about ourselves, and it drains us emotionally when we do. Remember, in developing prosperity consciousness, you will not only be up against your own resistance, but those of other people as well. Perhaps your parents or your mate will come up with some good reason why you can't possibly succeed at this, especially if they're insecure about your changing in some substantial way, or outstripping them. They may say things like, "This positive thinking stuff is too simple; it couldn't possibly work, and you're crazy to believe in it." Ignore these comments and just keep on making your affirmations. Better still, don't tell people who are likely to resist your efforts. Work in silence and accomplish your goals without having to use your energy convincing unbelievers. It isn't easy to stay positive when everyone around you is complaining about how broke they are. Don't listen to them! A mental trick I use when people try to give me negative ideas (or even when I catch myself saying them to myself) is to think *Cancel, Cancel!* and then immediately exchange the negative thought with a positive one.

Setting Your Goals

Deciding on your goals is the first step in your program. Once you make a decision to be rich, you have taken a giant step toward achieving it. But, before you can attain wealth, you must know exactly what you want and what you intend to do with it when you get it. People don't really want money—after all, it's just a piece of paper—they want what money can buy. Once you have a strong idea of what you intend to do with your money, you can begin to focus on the specific amount you will need each year to accomplish your desire. When you make your affirmations, don't just ask for enough to survive, ask for sufficient money to enjoy your life, such as traveling, buying a house, going to college, or getting some good stereo equipment. A friend of mind began making affirmations and told me that one of them was: "I will always have sufficient money to meet my needs." This is a limited concept and can result in just barely surviving. You want to do more than just meeting your essential needs. A better affirmation would be: "I will always have more than enough money to meet my needs and to enjoy my life."

Since the first requisite is to discover what you desire in life, where you are going, and what you intend to do when you get there, ask yourself: "How much money would I like to have each year to create my life the way I would like it?" Don't just read this question. Stop and take a moment right now to think about it. Make sure you know what you desire from life. Ask yourself this question: "How much am I worth an hour?" If you think it's only a few dollars, then that's all you'll ever get. You must begin by raising your own self-worth and self-value. Put a price on your time and skills that demonstrates their true worth, and don't downgrade yourself by underestimating the value of your time and energy. Your persistence, dedication, eagerness, loyalty, and conscientiousness are all worth money.

Remember, ideas form the foundation of all fortunes. Once you decide what you desire in life, you will have put into motion a force that will go out into the universe like a rocket, bringing back to you what you have asked for. The moment you choose your definite goal and start making affirmations, you will observe a strange circumstance; the ways and means of attaining it will begin immediately to reveal themselves. Any dominating desire, goal, or purpose held firmly in the conscious mind through imagery and repetition of thought is taken over by the subconscious mind and acted upon, and it is thus carried out to its logical conclusion by whatever means are available. The Creative Power Within will find the means.

Since the starting point of all achievement is adopting a definite purpose and a solid plan for its attainment, use the financial commitment statement on page 100 to write down three goals: those you wish to accomplish this year, those you will accomplish within five years, and your long-term, lifetime goals. Specifically state your goals even though these may not be totally clear at this point. By programming your subconscious to specific objectives, the means will reveal themselves. If the method of achieving them is not presently clear to you, write down dreams and fantasies about how you could make money. These could include, for example, writing a book, winning the lottery, being offered a new job at a larger salary, starting your own business, etc.

The purpose of this exercise is to start the wheels of your subconscious into motion by making a commitment. After you've jotted down your desire (or daydreams), make a plan to manifest it. State the maximum time allowed for each step of the plan and describe precisely what you intend to do to reach your objective. Make your plan flexible enough to permit changes at any time you are inspired to do so. Remember that the Creative Power Within may present you with a plan far superior to any you can presently envision. Be ready, therefore, to recognize and adopt any superior idea that may later be presented to your mind.

Make a copy of the Commitment Form (see page 100) and place it where you can see it regularly, then repeat it aloud at least once a day. If you have people who believe in you and in your ability to create whatever you want in life, tell them about your plan. Then they too can hold the image that your lifetime goals are coming true for you now.

Another way to impress the subconscious with your goals is to make a Treasure Map. After you have carefully thought out all the things you would like to do with the increase in money you are going to have, get a large sheet of posterboard. Begin looking through magazines and newspapers for pictures of your dreams. For example, an ad for the type of car you want, pictures of foreign lands, a cruise ship or plane flying to a dreamed-of vacation

Commitment Form

I, _____, on this _____ day of _____,
20___, hereby formally adopt the following financial goals:

By the end of this year, I will be earning at least $_____ per
month. Five years from this date, my yearly income will be at
least $_____. By the end of _____, my net worth will be at
least $_____. I intend to retire from my job by _____,
and devote my time to activities I enjoy, including:

_____

_____

_____

_____

_____

Some of the things I intend to do to manifest this plan are:

_____

_____

_____

_____

In order to accomplish the above goals, I pledge that I will spend
some time each day visualizing, and will make the following
affirmations:

_____

_____

_____

_____

_____

Signed: _____ Dated: _____

paradise, a beautiful new home, being a successful executive going to the office, a harmonious relationship (symbolized by a family having fun together, or sitting before a fireplace with your partner), or whatever appeals to you. Make a collage of your ideas and put it on a wall where you can look at it frequently. This further impresses your subconscious with the thought that this is coming true for you now, and you will give it life and power by doing this. Be sure to put yourself in the picture. Get a photo of yourself and of others you will want to have with you when you achieve prosperity, and paste them on the collage. You will then have taken a powerful step toward realizing your goal.

Using Affirmations to Attract Money

An affirmation is a strong, positive statement about something you want to manifest in your life. To affirm means to make something firm; thus, by stating your goal in a definite way, you make it more firm to your subconscious mind. Affirmations are positive signals you send to your brain every time you say them, so that through the law of attraction and vibration, your subconscious can begin working to provide you with whatever you want. Writing down affirmations is an extremely powerful technique for reaching deeply into the subconscious, and is the fastest way to incorporate these ideas into your consciousness. It is far more effective than simply stating your goals. Some of the most dramatic changes in my life have occurred through using affirmations. In fact, a few times the telephone has rung in the middle of my writing an affirmation, and it was the manifestation of what I had just written. The more you practice this technique, the more effective it will become for you.

The technique of using affirmations has been around for years. It's been taught in self-development courses and used by all positive thinkers and successful people. An excellent book on using affirmations to achieve prosperity consciousness is *Moneylove* by Jerry Gillies. I strongly recommend that you purchase this book.

Some of the affirmations in this chapter are from Gillies' book. Another wonderful book, now a classic, is Napoleon Hill's *Think and Grow Rich*.

Accentuate the Positive, Eliminate the Negative

Many people are not successful using affirmations because they already have so many negative ideas about themselves programmed into their subconscious minds that the positive affirmations cannot overcome them. Furthermore, they often don't know they harbor these false ideas, so they faithfully repeat affirmations that don't manifest because their negative past programming needs to be expunged first.

I learned this important point from Leonard Orr's money seminars. Orr discovered that all the negative material about money absorbed through the years must be dealt with before a person can become rich. Poverty consciousness, which may have been with you all your life, will dominate unless you remove all doubt so prosperity consciousness can get a firm foothold. The way to do this is to write down your positive affirmations and, while you are doing it, listen carefully to your body and your inner feelings for any negative thoughts that negate your affirmation. Write these down, too; then immediately refute them by writing down an opposite response. Keep on in this way until you can write the positive affirmation without getting any flak from your mind negating it. In this manner you can clear your mind completely of the negative ideas that make you think you don't deserve to be rich.

Here's an example of the kind of dialogue you might have with yourself:

> *I, [name], deserve to be wealthy and prosperous, and this is coming true for me now.*

> "Oh yeah, why should I be wealthy? I don't have any special talents, and I don't have a college degree."

You know very well that you don't have to have a degree to become rich. Henry Ford didn't finish high school, and neither did Tom Edison, or a lot of other prosperous people. And as for special talents, you really have plenty of them; you've just never had a chance to develop them. What about your writing ability and the paintings you did in high school that your teacher said were so good, and the pottery you've designed? Besides, you may think up something unique to sell that nobody has ever thought about before.

"Well, maybe you're right!"

I, [name], deserve to be wealthy and prosperous; and this is coming true for me now.

"Maybe I could sell something special or buy a small business. But Mom always said it wasn't important for women to make money because men don't want you to earn more than they do."

Really? What a limited concept! Are you going to depend on someone else all your life? What's wrong with having plenty of money of your own?

"Nothing."

I, [name], deserve to be wealthy and prosperous, and this is coming true for me now.

"Why should I deserve it when there are lots of people out there barely surviving?"

You deserve it because you're willing to take the time and energy to write these affirmations and gain control over your mind. You know that your subconscious will respond to whatever you program it with, so why not try it? Besides, your being poor isn't going to help all the other poor people.

> "Okay, I think you're right. I deserve it as much as any-
> one else, and I'm willing to work for it."
>
> *I, [name], deserve to be wealthy and prosperous, and this
> is coming true for me now.*
>
> "Hey—I think I'm beginning to believe this. I do deserve
> money!"

If, when using this technique, you get the same objection every time, invent an affirmation that is the opposite of that response. For instance, if you keep repeating, "I don't think I have any special talents," then write, "I deserve to be paid just for being the person I am," or "My special talents are now being revealed to me."

It's advisable to write your affirmations in three persons and always include your own name. Writing it in three persons has the effect of letting your subconscious mind think others also believe you deserve to be wealthy. For example:

> I, [name], deserve to be wealthy and prosperous, and this
> is coming true for me now.
>
> You, [name], deserve to be wealthy and prosperous, and
> this is coming true for you now.
>
> She, [name], deserves to be wealthy and prosperous, and
> this is coming true for her now.

Once you start actively reprogramming your subconscious, thereby becoming totally committed and emotionally involved in creating your own prosperity, you are sure to succeed. It's best to write a page of affirmations every day. Don't just do it by rote, but really think about and visualize in your mind's eye the meaning of the words you write. Notice your resistance, feelings of doubt, or negative thoughts; be sure to write them down, too. Then challenge the negative thoughts and counteract them with positive statements. In this way you will be able to discover why you have not been successful and how you have kept yourself from getting what you want. Once you feel that you've really overcome your negative programming, discontinue writing the negative and continue writing the positive.

The repetition of positive messages to your subconscious and the refuting of negative ones are the only foolproof ways to reprogram your brain. An actual chemical change takes place in the brain through repeated positive thinking. Poverty consciousness is always the result of ideas others have given you, while prosperity consciousness is the result of the ideas you give yourself. As you use this procedure, negative ideas you have buried in your subconscious will surface and be dealt with so you can clear your mind for wealth. It can save you years of trying to discover through psychotherapy why you can't succeed.

As a step in convincing your subconscious mind that you deserve to have money, Jerry Gillies suggests in *Moneylove* that you get a piece of paper, title it "Five Reasons Why I Deserve to Be Rich," and jot them down. We all have more talents and abilities than we usually acknowledge, and you probably have far more than your parents ever gave you credit for. Writing this down makes it more real to your subconscious mind.

Next, write down ten ways you can earn money. If you can think of ten ways you will succeed, you'll never be discouraged by temporary setbacks or by external conditions, such as high unemployment or the rate of inflation, and you'll never be broke. If you feel locked into a particular job and think you couldn't possibly do anything else, use this affirmation: *New opportunities for making money are opening to me daily.* Money can come from unexpected sources, and this affirmation takes away the restrictions on your earning potential. New vistas for making money surround you. By affirming this on a regular, daily basis, opportunities you have never even dreamed of will be placed in your path. The cooperation of others will become available to you, and job offers may suddenly appear as if by a stroke of magic. Your fears and doubts will disappear, and self-reliance and creativity will take their place. Somewhere along the way, the idea or the job for which you have been searching will reveal itself to you. That has been the experience of most people who use affirmations on a regular basis.

Patricia used affirmations very successfully. She came to me for counseling because she was very dissatisfied with her job as a secretary in a local electronics firm. She had worked for the company for six years, and was now at the top of her salary scale. As a single parent of three children, Patricia simply couldn't afford any luxuries, and was worried about meeting her obligations. She was tired of scrimping and wanted to explore other options so she could earn more money. We discussed her returning to college and getting a degree, but Patricia felt this was not practical with three small children. I taught her the technique of making affirmations, and she agreed to practice this faithfully, and to especially concentrate on writing this affirmation: *New opportunities for making money are opening to me daily.*

During December, Patricia brought me a beautiful dried flower arrangement as a Christmas gift. I admired the artistry, and Patricia shyly admitted that she made the arrangement herself. She had developed this hobby in order to have something to do with her hands when she was home with her kids watching television. I emphasized that she was extremely talented and encouraged her to think about opening a small business selling the floral arrangements. Not being in a financial position to quit her job, Patricia decided to clean out her garage and convert it into a flower shop. She had some business cards printed, got a license, set up a table, and began selling on the weekends. As her clientele grew and her self-esteem increased, she decided to take the plunge and applied for a small business loan to rent a store in a shopping plaza. Within a year she was making more money than she had ever earned as a secretary. An opportunity to make money, which she would never have dreamed of before, had presented itself to her as a result of her having diligently made affirmations, thus opening her subconscious mind to new possibilities.

Affirmations for Women

Women have often been given some very negative programming about money. In the past they were taught to believe from an early age they shouldn't attempt to make a lot of money because they'll always have a man to take care of them. How sad to groom our female children to be parasites, totally dependent on another person! Women have also been told that they will never make as much money as a man and they shouldn't bother trying. As a result, they often feel they don't deserve a high-salaried position and don't even strive for it. But highly motivated women can rise above the statistical world, which pays women some seventy cents for every dollar a man earns, and can bring into their lives whatever they wish through the power of their thoughts. Some excellent affirmations for women can be found in Shakti Gawain's beautiful book *Creative Visualization,* and Sondra Ray's *I Deserve Love.*

Here are some affirmations especially for women:

> I am a capable and successful person, and abundance is my birthright.

> I am a powerful, dynamic, and intelligent person, and I am manifesting my abundance now.

> I am self-confident, and my actions are decisive. I attract money to me through my desire to succeed.

> I deserve to be as successful as the most successful man, and this is coming true for me now.

> I am equal to the best of men, and there is no limit to my potential.

> I am entitled to a share of the world's wealth, and this is coming to me now.

The genius in me is being released, and I am now fulfilling my destiny.

I have enough time, energy, wisdom, and money to accomplish all my desires.

I expect the unexpected; my highest good now comes to pass.

There is an infinite number of possible affirmations. Adopt the ones most fitting to you. Be sure to personalize them to fit your particular situation.

Upgrading Necessity to Pleasure

I particularly like an affirmation used by Leonard Orr: *I work smarter, not harder.* Freedom is something we all want, and is probably one of the major goals of most working people. But, working just to accumulate enough money with which to retire is poverty consciousness, and you'll probably end up living on a pittance. It's like saying, "I don't deserve to have any freedom until I've put in so many years of hard labor"—just like a prison sentence. There is no reason why we should have to follow a Biblical injunction written over two thousand years ago, admonishing the people of that time to "earn your bread by the sweat of your brow." Many people are hooked to that concept. If that idea has been impregnated into your subconscious mind, the affirmation *I work smarter, not harder,* can change it.

One of the best things you can do for your own prosperity consciousness is to lift someone else's, so another important affirmation is: *The more I help others prosper, the more I prosper myself.* Money paid to others just means more money in circulation that can come back to you. A variation of this affirmation is: *A great deal of money is now coming into my life; I deserve it and will use it for my good and that of others.*

Many people are programmed to the idea that money is only for necessities, and it's frivolous or "unspiritual" to spend it for personal pleasure. If you feel this way, your life will be joyless and dull, and it's a good way to keep yourself in poverty. A life without fun, entertainment or vacations is not worth living and, as the saying goes, can "make Johnny a dull boy."

If you think spending money on yourself is immoral, you may have to work on programming yourself to the idea that part of the purpose of life is to enjoy it.

A friend of mine dated a man who was the classical stingy bachelor. Although Fred earned good money, he was extremely cautious about every penny he spent, and never bought any luxuries. He owned two suits, always ate at home, and refused to purchase birthday or Christmas gifts for his friends and family, which he considered frivolous. The money Fred saved with his miserly habits went into a passbook savings account at four-and-a-half percent interest. Since inflation was higher than that, Fred's money was slowly eaten up each year, guaranteeing he would end up as one of the many elderly people who barely subsist. He is a prime example of a person with poverty consciousness. Fred is probably still manifesting it to this day because he's too stingy to buy a book like this or attend a seminar on prosperity consciousness. His life is a joyless one.

The most effective way to live is to balance your necessary expenses with some pleasurable spending. Realize that some of your money is yours to keep, to spend on things you really enjoy. Remember, you're not working just to pay your bills, but also to enjoy your life. Because of their poverty consciousness, many people expand their expenses to meet their earnings so that there's never anything left over for pleasure. If your subconscious mind gets the message you only need money for necessities, it will arrange your affairs so that everything you earn goes for the basic things of life. So, take a step toward prosperity consciousness by taking some portion of your money every week, even if it's only five or ten dollars, and use it for yourself. Economizing all the time creates poverty consciousness. Learn to love yourself enough to realize you deserve the good things in life. To overcome the idea that you don't deserve pleasure, use one of these affirmations:

> A percentage of everything I earn is mine to keep for myself.
>
> My income now vastly exceeds my expenses.

While using this principle, at the same time be wise enough not to spend foolishly and indulge yourself in luxuries you don't need. Don't forget to regularly save a certain percentage of your income, which is equally important.

Personalizing Money

It's a good idea to personalize money instead of treating it as just a dirty piece of paper. That way you can develop an affinity for money that will attract it to you. For instance, you might think of money as a beautiful woman or handsome man who loves to visit you and can't get enough of you. In doing this, you could write:

> Money knows where I live, and she visits me daily.
>
> Money is a lover of mine, and I treat her kindly so that she comes to see me often.

Some people say they're really not interested in money, and pay little attention to it. If you're impersonal about money, it will be impersonal about you, and reject you. Everything in the universe has a life at some level, and money is no exception. Thus, make it into a reality in your life by giving it the respect you would give a dear friend or loved one. *"I love money, and money loves me."*

Increasing Your Prosperity Consciousness

Prosperity consciousness really is a spiritual idea, based on the principle that the Creative Power has provided infinite wealth, and a part of it is for our own personal use. There is a Power greater than the power of conscious thought, but usually it's not perceptible to our finite minds. Recognizing this truth is essential for the successful development of prosperity consciousness. No great enduring success has ever been achieved by those who do not recognize and use the spiritual powers of the universe. If you are connected with Spirit, you will find yourself with an abundance of opportunities to amass wealth, and it will never be at the expense of others.

Another good affirmation for increasing prosperity consciousness is: *My income increases every day whether I'm working, sleeping, or playing.* This is true because, if you have a savings account, even with only fifty dollars in it, your income is increasing every day because it's earning interest. It also means that you program your subconscious mind to give you valuable ideas each day so that your income will keep increasing. If you are working, most of your days involve a positive cash flow.

Make up a set of cards with your favorite affirmations printed on them and put them in an area where you can see them every day. You can put them on your refrigerator door, on the mirror in your bathroom, on the dashboard in your car, and on your bedroom nightstand. Even if you don't always read them, they'll be going into your subconscious mind every time you pass them and activate the brain cells connected with these positive thoughts. They will encourage and remind you of your own capacity for attracting money into your life.

A part of developing a prosperity consciousness is feeling good about yourself in general. Here are some affirmations you can use as needed:

Self-Confidence

I am completely relaxed, self-confident, and self-assured in everything I do.

I can accomplish any goal I desire through planning and self-motivation.

Concentration

I have the ability to focus my undivided attention on any particular task at any time. I am able to concentrate deeply on anything I set my mind to. I can shut out all distractions and focus my entire attention on the problem at hand.

Problem Solving

Every problem is an opportunity for me to be creative, and I am highly creative. I consider every problem that confronts me as a new door to be opened. I begin every job thinking of new and better ways to accomplish the task.

Relaxation

I am able to totally relax at will any time I wish. Regardless of the circumstances, I am a very relaxed and calm person, completely in control of myself.

Energy

I have all the energy I need for the day ahead. I am filled with rejuvenating life energy, and my total being is refreshed and energetic.

Composure

I am poised, relaxed, and peaceful. I accept challenges and disagreements with calmness.

Affirmations for Salespeople

I daily make valuable contributions to others by giving them an opportunity to own (name of product).

I am a friendly, pleasing person, and my customers like me.

I am highly disciplined and able to accomplish all of my daily plans.

People who enjoy my product are now being attracted to me.

Whenever people do not wish to buy my product, I never take it personally.

The more I sell, the easier it becomes to sell even more.

I enjoy my job and get great pleasure from dealing with my customers.

The great universal forces are now helping me to achieve my goals.

Affirmations are tools that can change your entire life, but if you don't use them, they don't work. You will not succeed if you constantly say, "Oh, I'm just too busy right now to sit down and do this." You must be willing to put the time and energy into this technique to experience the tremendous life changes that will begin taking effect once you do. You cannot begin this experiment and then immediately start checking yourself and say, "Wait a minute, I've written these for three days now, and so far I haven't received any money. This doesn't work." The subconscious never acts on a fleeting thought; it must be given constant programming until the ideas become firmly lodged in your mind and replace the negative ones already there. No enduring success will be achieved by those who are unwilling to put the necessary time and energy behind it. We must learn to think abundance constantly and hold steadily to constructive thought. It takes constant vigilance to gain supremacy over our unruly minds. The man or woman who will do this persistently and diligently is ensured of tremendous success in every area of life.

To honor the self is . . . to be in love with our own life, in love with our possibilities for growth and for experiencing joy, in love with the process of discovery and with exploring our distinctively human possibilities.

NATHANIEL BRANDEN, *To Honor the Self*

SEVEN
Attracting Love into Your Life

I once knew a very beautiful woman who was intelligent, charming, well-educated, and a good conversationalist, yet she always became involved with men who treated her very badly. Marcia was going through her third divorce when she came to me for counseling. Her first husband had been much older than she, and he totally dominated her. In their relationship, she played out the classic Freudian "Electra complex" by subconsciously trying to "get her daddy to love her." But it didn't work. Her father-substitute was so insecure because of her youth and beauty that he disapproved of her having any friends, occasionally followed her when she went on an errand, and refused to allow her to go to work in case she would meet a more desirable man at the office.

After five years of this domination, and increasing headaches and backaches, Marcia finally divorced him for the sake of her psychological and physical health.

Shortly thereafter, she was pursued by a man her own age who, she discovered too late, was addicted to cocaine. He had managed to conceal his habit so well that she was not aware of it until they had been married almost a year, and she became increasingly suspicious about missing money and jewelry. After a second divorce, and four years of single life trying to recover from this emotional shock, Marcia married a high-powered executive incapable of being faithful to her. He was also a periodic drunk, and would verbally abuse her in a sadistic fashion about once a month when on one of his binges.

Counseling with Marcia uncovered the fact that she subconsciously hated herself, and attracted men such as these because she thought it was what she deserved. Marcia came from a home where this beautiful, intelligent, sensitive woman had been treated as though she were a complete idiot, and was berated whenever she attempted to accomplish anything. Her parents' role seemed to be designed to demean and humiliate her, and she developed a severe inferiority complex. Little wonder then that she attracted men who reinforced her inner tape and "proved" she was an unworthy and unlovable person.

It is a cosmological law that people will treat you the way you treat yourself. If you hate yourself, you will not allow others to love you. When we have a low opinion of ourselves, we cannot accept the idea that someone can really love us; thus, we reject a person who does, in favor of someone who will abuse us and reinforce our feelings of inadequacy. We attract to ourselves those people and things in resonance with the type of vibrations we send out. Our ideas about our self-worth go out into the universe like a magnet and pull into our environment the type of person who conforms to our own inner image. In *Actualizations*, Stewart Emery writes: "If people's relationships with their own lives are unhappy, then their relationships with us are going to be unhappy as well. People who can't love themselves, can't love you either."

Perhaps, at the conclusion of a disastrous relationship, you have said to yourself: "I didn't know my partner was like that." Maybe you didn't on the conscious level, but the subconscious always knows and that area of the mind governs our lives. As Freud stated: "One subconscious mind understands another." At that level of awareness we know exactly what we are trying to accomplish, even if it is to destroy ourselves. If our old tapes are programmed for negative and destructive relationships, that's precisely what we'll get until we learn how to change those neurotic tapes.

Neurosis is perpetuated by the conflict between the idealized self (what one thinks one should be) and the real self, and represents the friction between desire and behavior, such as the following:

Desire	Behavior
Assert oneself appropriately	"Subassertiveness" or Aggressiveness
Get work done	Procrastinate
Stop bad habits	Addictions (overeating, drinking, etc.)
"Be this, be that"	"I can't do it"
	Resistance/Rebellion
	Self-destructive behavior (e.g., finding a mate who will abuse you)

Such behavior results in guilt, which leads to:

Lowered self-esteem, which results in:

Verbal abuse of yourself, such as thinking, "I'm worthless," thereby proving the negatively programmed tapes.

This self-hatred leads to:

Repression and denial, shutting down of feelings, inability to love others, fear of being in touch with loving feelings because of fear of rejection, loss of touch with the real self within because of fear of seeing what you don't like about yourself.

Neurosis is manifested by behaviors such as:

Conflict Radiating Inward

Depression

Anxiety

Sleep disorders

Chronic guilt feelings

Low self-esteem

Addictions (alcohol, drugs, food, etc.)

Psychosomatic illnesses (headaches, backaches, ulcers, heartburn, hypertension, etc.)

Conflict Radiating Outward

Chronic procrastination

Phobias

Defensiveness

"Subassertiveness"/Overly compliant

Victim behavior

Chronic dissatisfaction

Fear of intimacy

Fear of loss of control

Nervousness, panic states

Narcissism

Aggressiveness

Sense of isolation, alienation, and social withdrawal

Obsessive compulsive behaviors

For example, perfectionism: "I can't ever get it right; I can't ever relax."

Dependency
("I have to depend on you because I can't depend on
myself, and I resent you for it")

Helplessness
("Tell me what to do, but I'll resist it
and prove you wrong")

Indecisiveness
(fear of making a mistake)

Power Struggle
(hostile, hypercritical, punitive)

Excessive materialism
("I'm okay because of what I have")

If you were a victim of parents who didn't know how to love you and are thus limited in your ability to love others, as well as yourself, this can be changed through affirmations and mental imagery. If you were abused as a child, either verbally or physically, or find that you manifest a number of neurotic behaviors, you would be wise to seek professional counseling to assist you in deprogramming your parental tapes. But you can also help yourself, and thereby expand your ability to love.

The Nature of Self-Love

Self-love is not the same as egotism. The egotistical or narcissistic person really dislikes himself and has adopted an attitude of superiority as a defense against self-hatred. In our society, however, there is such a taboo against publicly expressing any type of love for oneself that some people are actually afraid to care about themselves. Notice, for example, how difficult it is for certain people to accept a compliment. They become embarrassed, tongue-tied, and try to avoid acknowledging it. If you truly care about yourself, you will always project this feeling to others in your environment. The essence of love is caring enough about yourself so that you can respect and care for others.

People will treat you the way you treat yourself, so begin to examine carefully the way you have been acting toward yourself. For example, think of someone you regard as a very good friend. When you are with this person, you probably tend to be solicitous, interested, respectful, protective, and loving toward him or her. You have the other person's best interests at heart and you care about them. Now ask yourself: "Do I give myself the same tender consideration? Do I treat myself as kindly and respectfully as I treat my friend?" On the basis of your self-evaluation, you may have to answer truthfully: "No, I don't!" If this is your answer, ask yourself "why?" Aren't you as important as your friend? Then treat yourself that way! Observe the messages you constantly give yourself. Do you call yourself names, bark orders at yourself, chastise and berate yourself when you have said or done something you consider inappropriate? If so, you only undermine yourself and decrease your self-esteem.

Many people are in conflict with themselves because one part of them is at war with another part. A useful way to deal with this inner conflict is to recognize that we all have three parts: our inner child of the past, our adult self, and the internalized parent who, most often, is critical of our behavior. Although we may outwardly look and behave like an adult, the other two parts are constantly influencing and governing our behavior, and they must be recognized and dealt with.

Adults who were the children of critical parents often have a very strongly developed, belittling inner parental voice governing them. As the psychiatrist Karen Horney pointed out, they are ruled by the "tyranny of should." They are constantly telling themselves, "I should do this," "I shouldn't have done that," "I should do better," "I shouldn't make mistakes," and so on. Recognizing, challenging, and questioning these dictates contributes greatly to freeing ourselves from the enslavement of our now internalized critical parent. At the same time, our inner child of the past, who is so often frightened and lonely, can be given reassurance by our adult part that we are really a worthy and lovable human being. Whenever you're feeling insecure, talk to the little child inside you, and let her know that you, the adult, really care about her. Mentally love, nurture, and console her. You'll be surprised how good this little exercise will make you feel.

As a child and a teenager, I constantly berated myself for just about everything. After being with a group of friends or going to a party, I would come home and immediately start critically judging my behavior. If I had done something I considered dumb or socially incorrect, I called myself names for days and continually reminded myself of my ineptitude. Finally, I realized my self-condemnation was so severe I was making myself into a hopeless neurotic. I began to think of my critical, internalized parent as a person looking over my left shoulder, following me around and constantly belittling me. I vowed to get control of it, and put an end to this terrible guilt and self-condemnation.

I started my transformation by making a bargain with myself that I would allow myself to correct something I had done, once and only once. Once is a learning experience; anything after that is nagging and berating. So I began by labeling certain behaviors as inappropriate, rather than dumb, stupid, childish, or disgraceful, and told myself that I had now learned not to say or do that and had no need to repeat it. It became a corrective process, not a mental beating. After that, whenever the inner parent began to criticize me, I turned around and screamed "Shut up!" at the top of my voice, unless, of course, if I were in public, then I screamed it in my mind. This may sound like a silly thing to do, but within three weeks I had gained total control over my self-condemnation and never again allowed my tyrannical inner parent to degrade or humiliate me.

Let's begin with a method for raising self-esteem. The first principle in your program to increase self-esteem is . . .

Always talk kindly to yourself

Treat yourself as you would a loving friend and never, never call yourself names or denigrate yourself for inappropriate actions. As a therapist, I often assign homework to clients to give themselves a compliment every day. For some people, this is very difficult; they simply can't think of anything about themselves that they like. How can we expect others to like us when we don't like ourselves? You can learn to become a loving friend to yourself and, even though you may not like some of your behaviors, you can always love your own inner self that is striving so hard to become a well-adjusted, self-actualizing person. In fact, with some people who are very lonely and have no one to love them, I ask them to repeat a statement every morning the moment they wake up, even before they open their eyes: "I love you, _____ (their name); you're a wonderful person." If you feel unloved, you will be amazed at how this simple affirmation will change your feelings about yourself. It's as though your higher self—that something deep within you—recognizes, respects, and loves you. It's a marvelous way to begin each day! When you have a need for love, you can begin by supplying it within yourself.

Give yourself at least one compliment every single day

Instead of relying on others to say you are doing a good job, or that they like the way you've done something, or the outfit you're wearing that day, do it yourself. This will help boost your self-esteem and you won't be disappointed if others fail to notice certain things. Every time you accomplish something, be it small or great, pat yourself on the shoulder and compliment yourself. Be proud of yourself and acknowledge your efforts, then you won't be dependent on others to compliment you.

A man once told me that he had cured himself of a painful back condition by simply placing his hand on his lower back several times a day and repeating, "I love you, back. You're a part of me and I will take care of you the best I can." The pain began gradually disappearing. How different this is from the approach most people take! Usually we hate the part of us that is giving us trouble, and would be rid of it if we could, thereby concentrating negative energy on that area.

Acknowledge and praise yourself verbally

No one can live without some feeling that they are a lovable and worthy person. You can use some of the following affirmations to raise your self-esteem.

> I, [Name], like myself. I am a lovable person.
>
> I now feel loved and appreciated by my parents, my friends, and everyone who is important to me. (Even if you don't, repeated use of this affirmation will soon cause it to be true!)
>
> My days are filled with love, joy, and abundance.
>
> I now give and receive love freely.
>
> I deserve to be loved, and I am a lovable person.

Here are a few affirmations that are especially effective for developing self-esteem, from Shakti Gawain's wonderful book *Creative Visualization*.

> Every day I am growing more beautiful and more radiantly healthy!
>
> The more I love and appreciate myself, the more beautiful I am becoming.
>
> I am now irresistibly attractive to men (or women).
>
> I am kind and loving, and I have a great deal to share with others.

In addition to writing these or similar affirmations, make it a point to do something nice for yourself every day. It need not be something that costs a lot of money, such as buying a new outfit, but some simple pleasure that makes you feel good about yourself and nurtures your spirit. This may be soaking in a bubble bath, taking a walk, window shopping, reading a favorite novel, taking the time to watch the sun set, or just listening to some beautiful music you enjoy. Nurture yourself in the same way you would like someone else to take care of you. When you feel loved inside, you make room in your heart for love to come to you.

Overcoming Procrastination

Chronic procrastination is one of the most common self-defeating behaviors exhibited by people who have difficulty loving themselves. Many people cannot do what needs to be done because they use punitive measures and try to beat themselves into action mentally, and thus hook their rebellious inner child who refuses to cooperate. People who were coerced as children often learn procrastination as a defense, and as a way of gaining some power in a powerless situation. Mother yells: "Get in here this very minute! Wash your hands right now! I want that room cleaned up immediately!" The child may not be able to refuse to do it, but she can take as much time as possible to fulfill the task. "Okay, mom, I'll do it as soon as this program is over. I'm coming, Mom. Just one more minute and I'll come in."

In this subtle way the child rebels against such domination. Then, in later life, when the same person attempts to get his bills paid on time, clean out the closet, complete his income tax forms, etc., he yells at himself internally in the very same tone of voice used by the domineering parent. So what happens? He rebels and procrastinates until the very last minute, and sometimes beyond that, and his life gets into a mess. This is, of course, self-defeating behavior, which perpetuates self-hatred. He hates himself for being this way, but he's powerless to stop, because this neurotic behavior is driven by his inner child of the past, with whom he has never adequately dealt.

An essential element of self-esteem is the judgment we make about ourselves because of what we accomplish. Taking care of the things in our lives we tend to put off helps build self-esteem. If you constantly procrastinate, you give yourself plenty of opportunity to consider yourself incompetent or a failure. Routinely taking care of things is a way of clearing your mind and having more energy, because you're not tying up a portion of that energy by holding something in the back of your mind that has to be done. By handling everyday tasks, you are handling your life; and it will convince your mind that you are an adequate person. Taking care of these tasks is a way of *being here now,* and living in the present. To free your mental energy, begin doing the tasks you have avoided, and an increase in self-esteem will automatically follow as a result of your accomplishments.

Here is a systematic way to deal with chronic procrastination. Take a piece of paper and list on it the five most important things in your life that have to be done. To begin with, preferably choose the simplest. Then, estimate the length of time it will take you to do this project. A task can often be facilitated just by figuring out how long it's going to take. You may be surprised to discover that there are some items on your list that can be completed in fifteen minutes or a half-hour that you have been putting off for weeks, and needlessly tying up energy by worrying about it. Next, ask yourself: "Why haven't I finished this task yet?" List as many reasons as you can think of. You probably have a mental picture that the task is very unpleasant, perhaps even painful, or so huge that it seems overwhelming. Or perhaps you are uncertain that you have the skills to accomplish it. If so, write this all down.

In a new column, list the solutions to each one of the stated obstacles. If you don't think you have enough information to complete the task, write down who you will have to contact or where you will have to go to acquire the information. Then list the benefits you expect to receive as a result of completing this task.

These may be internal, for example, increased self-esteem, a feeling of accomplishment, freedom from worry, more time for play. Or, you may also accrue some external benefit, such as praise from others or additional income. Writing down these benefits will help increase your motivation. Next, list the steps you need to take to complete the task. Break these down into very small steps. What is the first thing you need to do to approach this task? Get out some papers, go into your desk, open the closet door, get some boxes for storage? List *everything* you need to do. When you've written down all the steps, determine how long each step will take. Then write a date of anticipated completion beside each step. If you have a large task that will take an entire weekend, such as cleaning out the garage, it's best to spread the work over several Saturdays. You probably can't motivate yourself to spend the whole weekend working in the garage, so make a realistic schedule, such as 1 to 5 P.M. every Saturday for the next three weeks. Remember, set yourself up to win!

Now, use your imagination. Take a few minutes to relax and visualize yourself doing the task and completing it. This point is very important to increase your motivation. You may want to see yourself telling someone that you've completed it, and see them being pleased by this. Or you might visualize yourself standing back and admiring how nice the garage or closet looks now that you've cleaned out all the junk. Notice how good you feel when your project is accomplished. This is one of the most significant parts of the program because if you can accomplish the task in your mind, you will find it much easier to accomplish it in reality.

Finally, choose a reward you can give yourself when you have completed the project. It need not be something large, but it's very important to reinforce your efforts by rewarding yourself. Photocopy the worksheet on page 127 to assist you in systematically overcoming procrastination. It will go a long way toward increasing your self-esteem!

Overcoming Procrastination Worksheet

1. The *Most Important Task* for me to do this week is:

_____

2. I will *Begin* this task on:

_____

3. Estimated *Total Length of Time* to do task:

_____

4. *Reasons* why I haven't done it so far:

_____

_____

_____

_____

5. *Solutions* to each of the above reasons:

_____

_____

_____

_____

6. *Steps* to complete task: Length of time (each step)

_____

_____

_____

_____

7. *Benefits* I will acquire from completing task:

_____

_____

_____

_____

8. *Visualize working and completing* the task. Get the feeling of its completion.

9. On completion, I will *Reward* myself in the following way:

_____

Signed: _____ Dated: _____

Attracting Love

The most important ingredient for attracting love is learning to live with, by, and for yourself first. If you are single, you can create the conditions for love by being a loving person to yourself and others. Instead of a time of loneliness and pain, being single can be a time devoted to self-development. It's the best way to develop your own inner resources and really get to know who you are at the deepest levels of your being. Being alone can be a time of self-discovery and self-renewal if you see the possibility for such growth, and it's an opportunity to gain new certainty about yourself.

Being single is a great challenge and helps develop the inner strength necessary to face life fully as a strong, independent individual. When a person merges with someone else they can lose sight of their true self and begin living through the other person. Someone who has developed his or her own resources and skills is usually far more interesting than a person who has lived in the shadow of another. When the right partner arrives, he or she will have something to give and something to share. She becomes a whole person who is unified within her own center, and others will recognize and appreciate that.

Love, like other things in life, can be consciously produced. Just as you can make affirmations to increase your prosperity, so can you attract into your life the type of person you desire, using the same procedure. Here again, the laws of the universe apply. You must be careful not to violate cosmic law by manipulating the will of another. Therefore, make affirmations for the type of person you want, but *never specify a particular individual.* Leave that to Spirit and, if it is cosmologically right for you to have a certain person, that will surely happen. On the other hand, if you try to force it through the power of your thought, you may succeed in attracting a particular individual, but there will always be some backlash, in accordance with the cosmic law of cause and effect.

The first thing to do before making affirmations for love is to get a clear picture in your mind of exactly the type of person you desire. This seems self-evident but, believe it or not, many people never consciously think about the specific characteristics of a person who would be most harmonious with their personality. It's a good idea to get out a piece of paper and write these down. If you have difficulty, begin by thinking of your own qualities and make a list of those. Would you like your mate to have similar qualities, or would you prefer the opposite to counterbalance yours? For example, if you tend to be a spendthrift, you may want someone who is good at handling money, who can help curb your excessive habits. If you like classical music, you would probably prefer someone who also does; otherwise, his or her love of hard rock could drive you crazy. If you're athletic, it's best to specify someone who shares this interest, rather than a person who wants to stay home and read a book or watch television.

Additionally, be sure to list inner qualities you would like in your mate, such as honest, warm and loving, loyal, kind, thoughtful, growth-oriented, mature, spiritually-inclined, financially stable, or any other attributes that appeal to you. Since this is such an important part of your affirmations, you may want to take some time to really meditate about the type of person you desire. Remember, the more specific you can be, the easier it is for your subconscious to fulfill your desire.

Another important question to ask before writing your affirmations is, "What is my objective?" Do you want to be married, or would you rather just live with someone for a period of time? Are you looking for a long-term, permanent involvement, or just a temporary relationship? Perhaps you are so immersed in building your career right now that all you want is a fun-loving person to share some good times with, who is also looking for the same level of involvement. Are you the type of person who expects total fidelity and is willing to give the same to your partner? If so, list fidelity or loyalty as one of the qualities you want. Do you expect a monogamous marriage or would you prefer an open relationship with both parties able to see others? If you want marriage, do you want children? If you do, you should specify that you desire a mate who also wants children.

Be sure you have everything you want in your affirmations, but at the same time recognize your limitations. If you don't have the face and figure of a high fashion model, you're not likely to attract the equivalent of Hollywood's current Adonis. No one is perfect, but there is a human tendency to think that we can attract superstars, thus rejecting people who don't measure up to the fantasized image of what we want. When you have completed your list, look it over and ask yourself if it's realistic. For instance, if you want a woman who is slender, blonde, and beautiful, president of a large corporation, intelligent, educated, charming, and wealthy, then appraise yourself realistically to see if you would have enough to offer such a person.

Laura, a former client of mine, illustrated the importance of specifying everything you want in a mate. She divorced her husband of ten years because he was lazy, boring, and impotent. For seven of their ten years together, he had been almost totally uninterested in sex and wouldn't seek help for his problem. So, when she began her affirmations, she focused on her primary interest of having a good sexual relationship. That's exactly what she got; a man who was extremely virile and able to please her sexually. But she soon discovered he also wanted to please other women, and didn't believe in monogamy. For two years she was distraught every time she caught him with someone else, and that did more damage to her self-esteem than ten years with her uninteresting husband. Finally, she could take it no longer. She decided the sexual satisfaction wasn't worth the mental abuse, and saved what little self-respect she had left by leaving him. At this point she almost lost her job because of her inner turmoil, and had to seek psychotherapy to restore her confidence in herself. Before beginning affirmations for a more satisfactory partner, she worked for several months on a program to develop her self-esteem, and convince herself that she was a worthy person and deserved better than she'd had.

An interesting book containing many affirmations for finding a partner is Sondra Ray's *I Deserve Love,* and some of the following affirmations were designed by her. Though these samples are all written in the first person, remember to put your own name into these. You should also write them in three persons: I, you, and she or he. When you write your affirmations in the second and third persons, it gives you the feeling that "someone out there" also believes that you can have what you desire, and further impresses your subconscious mind.

> I, Dorothy, deserve love, and the type of man I desire is coming to me now. He will be interesting, kind, warm and loving, faithful, financially stable, thoughtful, educated, emotionally mature, and he will like children.

> I, Marc, deserve love, and the type of woman I desire is coming to me now. She will be intelligent, attractive, considerate, loving, athletic, interested in rock music, and able to move if I'm transferred.

> I, Joanne, am now attracting a man who is tender, kind, responsible, intelligent, successful, open, and who has a sense of humor.

> I, Paul, am now attracting a woman who is affectionate, passionate, interested in my kids, confident, joyful, and desires to stay at home and take care of the family.

> I, Patricia, am filled with loving thoughts and magnetic power so that I can draw to myself the right type of relationships. There is an abundance of lovers who are just right for me, and I am attracting them to me now.

> I, Larry, am now attracting into my life someone humorous and pleasurable, someone I can have fun with.

You can also specify approximately when you will meet the person you desire:

> I, Jeannie, am now sending out the mental vibration of love, and the type of person I desire will be attracted to me. I will meet him this spring, and we will be married by the end of the year.

> I, Bob, am now being led to the places where I will meet the type of person I desire. The universal law is now working so that I will be in the right place at the right time. My true love is now being attracted to me. We will buy a house together and be married by Christmas.

Listening to Your Inner Voice

Sometimes people have difficulty attracting love because they are not really ready to be involved with someone. This can be for a variety of reasons, such as being too busy to dedicate themselves to someone else. To discover any hidden thoughts that may be preventing you from finding love, you should divide your paper in half; use one side for the positive affirmations and the other side for writing down any negative or counter-thoughts you may have. Listen carefully to your body while you are writing and notice if you get any negative reaction. If you do, write these down, and challenge them by writing counter-affirmations.

For instance, Barbara began writing:

> I, Barbara, now have the time and energy for a permanent, monogamous relationship, and this is coming true for me now.

Every time she wrote this, she could feel her stomach muscles tightening up. So, using the other half of the page, she wrote this dialogue with herself:

Oh yeah? You're far too busy developing your career to devote your time to someone else.

That may be, but I'm very lonely, and I want a permanent, monogamous relationship and this is coming true for me now.

Stop kidding yourself. You couldn't handle it. He'll be demanding of your time, and you'll resent it.

Maybe you're right. I guess it's just the wrong time for me to try for a long-term goal. I'd better concentrate on my career first.

This mental dialogue led Barbara to revise her affirmation to:

I, Barbara, deserve love, and I am now attracting into my life someone I can have fun with, who has his own projects and won't be too demanding of my time.

Affirmations to Overcome Fear of Love

Sometimes people cannot attract a new love because they have been hurt in the past, and are afraid it may occur again. If this is preventing you from finding an appropriate partner, use some of the following affirmations:

I, _____, am now free of the past regarding my negative emotional experiences. I have learned a great deal from them and will not repeat the same mistakes.

I, _____, no longer focus on the losses I have suffered in the past. Instead, I am confident that my next relationship will be a beautiful and harmonious one.

I, _____, deserve to have someone who will love me exclusively, and the type of person I desire is being attracted to me now.

I, _____, forgive _____ for the way (she/he) treated me, and I am now releasing this experience into the universe and will no longer suffer from it.

I, _____, do not need to get even with men (or women) any longer. I can let them love me.

I, _____, am willing to accept love and stop resisting. It is safe to surrender to love.

I, _____, now take full responsibility for my actions, so I no longer feel guilty for anything I have done in the past.

I, _____, am no longer angry at women (or men). I feel very loving towards them, and am now attracting a loving person into my life.

I, _____, am now releasing my past experience with _____ and am no longer affected by it.

I, _____, still have love in my heart for _____, but since (she/he) is no longer interested in me, I am now completely accepting of this and wish (him/her) well in the new relationship.

You Deserve Love

Many people are hampered in their ability to find a loving mate simply because they don't believe they deserve one. If you feel this way, use your affirmations to convince your subconscious mind you are worthy of love.

Beverly, a lesbian, made an appointment with me because she felt so unworthy she had been unable to find a lover for three years. Five years prior to that she lived with a woman who suddenly decided she could no longer handle the enormous difficulties of being gay in a society that condemns those who love people of the same gender. Beverly's former lover lived in fear of being discovered, losing her job, and having family and friends turn against her. Finally, she told Beverly she wanted to end the relationship, get married to a man, and try to live a "normal" life without deception. Beverly was devastated by this and felt suicidal. In her despair, she went home and revealed to her parents for the first time that she was a lesbian. Tragically, they were horrified by this revelation, told her she was an "abomination before the Lord," and said they never wanted to see her again.

Because of her deep feelings of unworthiness and her fear of being hurt again in a relationship, Beverly was unable to find another woman to love. During psychotherapy she fought hard to regain her dignity and self-respect as a person, even though her lifestyle was different from the majority. She came to realize that what was important was not how others viewed her, but how she viewed herself. She knew that she was not "less than human" because she loved women, and decided that she had to be true to her own inner self, and not the dictates of others. Once her inner conflicts were resolved and she could accept herself, she began making positive affirmations for love, and found a new relationship within a few months.

Overcoming Negative Programming

If you have been the victim of negative concepts as a child, such as: "you're stupid," "why can't you be like your big brother," "you're really awkward and clumsy," "you won't amount to a hill of beans," etc., use the following affirmations to change these suggestions. Remember, you must find as many reasons as possible why you deserve love so your subconscious mind will be reprogrammed to the idea that you are really worthy.

Try some of the following:

> I deserve love because I am a warm and loving person and have helped many people in my lifetime.

> I deserve love because I have a great deal of love to give and am willing to share it.

I deserve love because I have a lot of personal assets and really care about people.

I deserve love because I have had a great deal of suffering in my life, and I don't intend to suffer any more.

I deserve love just because I am alive, and I'm entitled to happiness.

I think highly of myself and therefore it is easy for people to love me.

I now feel secure about my ability to attract the type of person I desire, and I deserve the best.

I deserve love because I am a loving person.

Affirmations, done consistently, can help create your life exactly as you truly desire it to be—happy, prosperous, healthy, fulfilling, joyous, creative and, particularly, filled with love. By reprogramming your barriers to love, both consciously and subconsciously, you can enjoy the complete fulfillment and satisfaction that always accompanies real love.

The most beautiful and most profound emotion we can experience is the sensation of the mystical. It is the power of all true science. . . . To know that what is impenetrable to us really exists, manifesting itself as the highest wisdom and the most radiant beauty which our dull faculties can comprehend only in their most primitive form—this knowledge, this feeling, is at the center of true religiousness.

ALBERT EINSTEIN

EIGHT
Guidance from Your Higher Self

Although this book presents a variety of methods for achieving success in life, it must be remembered that true happiness does not come from material possessions, prestige, power, or status. Many who have gained all of these have been very lonely, troubled individuals. Deep and lasting fulfillment can come only from developing a harmonious relationship with your inner self. The first step, always, is to work at becoming the person you want to be. The things you want to have in your life will follow automatically.

We live on four planes: the physical, mental, emotional, and spiritual. All these aspects of our existence must be nurtured and cared for if we are to become psychologically healthy, self-actualizing human beings.

The needs for meaning, for higher values, for a spiritual life, are as real as biological and social needs. Two great psychiatrists, Roberto Assagioli, author of *Psychosynthesis,* and Carl Jung, strongly stressed the need to develop our higher psychic functions, the spiritual dimension of our lives, since this awareness leads to wholeness, security, and joy.

What we are experiencing in this technological age is an impoverishment of our spiritual selves. We are living in a society surfeiting us with "things" we are constantly urged to purchase, yet offering us little to nourish the higher, aesthetic side of our nature, so the inner self is often parched and neglected. We have evidence of this in the enormous number of neurotic and unhappy people we see around us, many of whom are consuming a tremendous quantity of prescription and nonprescription drugs, alcohol, and other substances, to mitigate their emotional pain. We have to realize—and often life forces us to realize—that the spiritual aspect of our personality must be nourished, and is as vital to our lives as food and water. "To not give credence to the spiritual life," Albert Einstein once stated, "is to deny the validity of human experience."

It is really not possible to live an emotionally healthy life without making some contact with our inner self. We can develop our personality, our intellect, our physical body, and our career, but eventually we must satisfactorily answer the deepest, most fundamental questions of life if we are to actualize our full potential as human beings—the most advanced creatures on earth. "What is the meaning of my life?" "What is my purpose and ultimate goal?" These questions are basic to living a joyous, harmonious life, yet they are the very questions our academic institutions largely ignore. Thus, our schools and universities are graduating students who know how to program computers and analyze data, but who know very little about how to live a life constructively and gain the greatest fulfillment from it.

We are all aware that we have five outer senses—hearing, seeing, smelling, tasting, and touching—that bring us information about the external world. But we are often unaware that we also have inner senses, such as intuition, imagination, perception, clairvoyance, and other faculties that can be categorized as extrasensory perception. Civilization has chosen to ignore these inner senses, so they have become diminished through neglect. Yet, there is a wealth of hidden knowledge within the subconscious realm of our minds, to which we could avail ourselves if we would only listen. All of our faculties can be consciously developed, stimulated, and augmented because they are in a state of *becoming,* either developing or diminishing as we grow older, depending upon the amount of attention we give to them.

To expand our consciousness and begin to live in a higher dimension, we must develop these intuitive faculties. They will start to open up by a natural process when we consciously attempt to live a higher life and express the positive emotions, such as love, joy, and compassion. Though many people today have a smattering of extrasensory capacity, most have not developed their spiritual consciousness. On the other hand, it's unfortunate that some so-called psychic people are misusing their gift as an ego trip by pretending they have something that others don't, and cashing in on it. I cannot emphasize strongly enough that the gift of intuitive power is available to all of us when we are open to receive it.

The Importance of Meditation

One of the most fundamental methods of developing and expanding the higher faculties is meditation, the single most important pathway to higher consciousness. Through regular and persistent meditation, the voice of intuition speaks to us to guide and help our lives. But people often avoid meditation, claiming it is too difficult to learn the correct method. Is there a correct method? Is it necessary to take courses in specific techniques and learn intricate disciplines before you can meditate in the most appropriate way? I would answer these questions by echoing the great Indian teacher Krishnamurti: "Do not ask me how to meditate, do it!" Meditation can begin with the simplest of questions: "Who am I?" And then listen to the thoughts that follow. Or: "I am an expression of the Infinite. How has Spirit chosen to express itself through me?"

In his wonderful book *Learn to Meditate,* David Fontana says "Meditation . . . is the most profound method of exploring the mind, and plumbing the mysteries of being, known to humankind. . . . Like a journey during which every turn of the road opens up new vistas, meditation reveals insight after insight as it takes us ever deeper into ourselves." By acquainting us with ourselves on the deepest level, meditation enriches our lives in a way no other discipline can.

When meditation becomes habitual, a permanent change takes place in one's life, and one begins to perceive the existence of something beyond the five senses. As you become more spiritually minded, you will realize that the inner strength you can build during meditation will help you to overcome any problem in your life. Every time you practice meditation, you make a gain that becomes a soul-possession and a soul-profit forevermore.

History records that the most highly evolved lights of this world, such as Socrates, Plato, Walt Whitman, Mary Baker Eddy, and Saint Teresa of Avila, all spent a great deal of time contemplating inwardly, getting in touch with their higher nature, which is the only way to self-realization. These great souls were, for the most part, solitary individuals; men and women who walked alone, thought alone, and communed with nature alone. In solitude, each came to grips with the meaning of his or her life and the direction it should be channeled. It is in these moments of solitude that we can discover our inner self, and realize the true nature of our relationship with life.

Most people run away from the challenge of being with themselves by attempting to find themselves through someone else.

People who are afraid to be left in isolation with themselves surround their lives with constant noise and distractions, thereby
drowning out the still, small voice within. If, instead of running
away, you will spend some time with yourself, you will have the
joyous experience of discovering who you really are at the deepest levels of your being. To make room for a deeper understanding, the ego has to be moved over. The only way to do this is to
have sufficient time and silence to allow Spirit the opportunity to
speak to your mind and heart. Unless we make some room in
our consciousness for Spirit to incline us from within, we cannot
hear Its guiding voice.

It is not necessary to turn away from the world by hiding in a
monastery or Himalayan cave to achieve this attitude. One can
learn to remain in the midst of conflict and confront it for what
it is, yet maintain one's serenity. Meditation is not a withdrawal
from the world; it is a return to reality, but it's a different view of
reality. Real happiness comes from struggling with the difficult
and overcoming it, not avoiding it. People who live what may be
called the contemplative life, or the spiritual life, do not allow
their inner peace to be disturbed by all the confusion and disso-
nance of the outer world—and that's what makes their lives different. As Dr. Thurman Fleet has said: "Nothing is worthy of
disturbing your inner peace." Adopting this philosophy is a
wonderful, serene way to live, regardless of outer circumstances.
As Thomas Merton states in *The Seven Storey Mountain:*

> The contemplative person ceases to identify himself with
> the actions that are contributing to the problems, to the
> violence, to the madness of the mob. He watches the play
> but he is not emotionally involved in it. Yet at the same
> time he is not under the delusion that he is better than
> those who are involved in it. It is not the world that is
> bad, but the way of being in the world which kills that
> which is most vital in man if he becomes enslaved to it.
> And then one experiences within oneself the entrapment

of the Spirit, or the separation of the lower nature from the higher . . . and the person has lost himself. One who is free from the controlling domination of his emotions is the only one who can think intelligently. Since he is not governed solely by his passions, he can see clearly, and thus he acts clearly from this standpoint of self-mastery.

Meditation is a powerful technique for transformation and requires no elaborate preparation, so you can begin using this technique right now, even before you finish reading this book. To assist you, here are some simple steps that will create the appropriate mood. Fundamental to successful meditation is finding a quiet place, with no distractions. Plan to meditate fifteen minutes to a half-hour when you begin. Later, as you start to experience the benefits accrued from this quiet time, you may wish to extend it. Be sure you will not be disturbed by the telephone, the kids, or the dog, because if you're concerned about being interrupted, it will interfere with achieving maximum introspection. It will be especially helpful if you have a separate room you can use at this time; if not, reserve a special chair for use only when you are meditating. This helps trigger a "conditioned reflex" whenever you sit in that chair, which is conducive to your intention.

It is best to meditate with the lights off and your eyes closed. If this bothers you, however, simply dim the lights so they will not be distracting. Begin your meditation by relaxing your body as much as possible. If you wish, you can use the relaxation formula given in Appendix A (see page 205) to accomplish this.

When you first begin to meditate, it will probably require a week or two to train your mind to focus on the task at hand. The mind is a great trickster, and often brings up things you would least like to think about at the beginning of meditation. If you are already accustomed to meditating but have stopped practicing it for a period of time, you'll probably find that it takes a week or two to get back in tune with it. Whether you are a novice or a former practitioner, have patience—the rewards are great!

I like to divide my meditation period into two parts, one I call *concentration* and the other *decentration,* or the active and passive parts of my session. In the active part, after calming my body and mind, I spend five to ten minutes making visual images and affirmations for things I want to achieve in my life. When I feel this is complete, I begin the passive part of my meditation, during which the inspirational thoughts and deeper effects occur. This is the time when you attempt to move your ego-self out of the way to listen quietly to your inner voice. At this stage, you must shut down the machinery of your mind as much as possible and simply allow thoughts, flashes of intuition, and guidance from Spirit to come to you. This can be a time of sublime joy, a time when you make contact with the Infinite and feel a peaceful, blissful unity with all life. This is the ecstasy spoken of by mystics and saints and, though rare, is the greatest benefit of meditation and its highest achievement. It is available to anyone willing to put in the necessary time and effort.

To achieve this state, you need a method for stilling the numerous thoughts of the mind. The best way of doing this is either to concentrate on your breathing or choose a "mantra," a single, meaningless sound on which to focus. Transcendental Meditation masters give students a particular Sanskrit word upon which they concentrate to clear the mind. Dr. Herbert Benson, author of *The Relaxation Response,* found that the word "One" is equally effective.

I have found that concentrating on slowing down my breathing as much as possible, accomplishes the same objective. One way is to breathe in slowly to the count of eight, hold your breath for a count of eight, then breathe out slowly to the count of eight. There must be no strain whatsoever in doing this; if eight counts are difficult for you to hold, try a smaller count until you feel comfortable. Continue breathing this way until your body feels almost motionless and your mind is equally stilled. Once still, a feeling of peace, harmony, and oneness will often flood your being. Sometimes intuitive insights and messages from the subconscious will accompany this, or they may just flash into your mind at a later date.

The most effective way to achieve self-mastery is through meditation. The inner strength you gain will help you overcome any lack in your life, and you will find the time of peaceful meditation not only inspiring but a great benefit to your physical and emotional well-being. Researchers have demonstrated that meditation can reduce hypertension, eliminate headaches, and alleviate a variety of other medical problems.

Through regular meditation you come continuously closer to alignment of the self with the Infinite Wisdom and Creative Power Within. Through meditation you can achieve a greater sense of the spiritual and cosmic nature of your life by turning your consciousness to your Higher Self. It is invaluable to the evolution of your consciousness and, in fact, is the only way to discover Spirit Within and reawaken the eternal within you. Once you are in contact with your Higher Self, anything is possible to you. The pathway to love, security, and inner peace is reached by integrating all the aspects of yourself—spiritual, mental, emotional, and physical. Make continuous efforts to contact Spirit, thus awakening your Higher Self, which will guide and direct you in achieving your goals in life. It is a beautiful, noble, loving way to live, and it will bring you total fulfillment.

> You ask me where I get my ideas, that I cannot tell you with certainty; They come unsummoned, directly, indirectly—I could seize them with my hands—out in the open air; in the woods, while walking; in the silence of the night; early in the morning, incited by moods, which are translated by the poet into words, by me, into tones that sound and roar and storm about me until I have set them down in notes.
>
> LUDWIG VAN BEETHOVEN

Thoughts and mental images are capable of initiating physiologic changes in your body. You can control your own thoughts; you can heal yourself just as you learned to make your body walk. The key is to picture your body normalized.

DR. IRVING OYLE, *The Healing Mind*

NINE
Self-Healing
Through Visualization

The human body, unlike a machine, has the ability to heal itself, and the source of its healing power is under the control of your mind, which can cause disease or create health. The great majority of diseases are psychosomatic, meaning that the origin is in the mind, and the result is in the body. If we can be psychosomatically ill, why can't we be psychosomatically *healthy?*

If, through stress or negative thinking, you have created a "*dis*-ease" in your body, you can also create the conditions that will allow the healing process to occur. Much disease is caused by incorrect thinking patterns, radiating their negative energy within the body. If you change these unhealthy beliefs and emotions, you can literally rebuild your body by rebuilding your thinking. The amazing fact about the body is you already have the healing power within you that is far more powerful than any form of external treatment! The most advanced medications available today can only approximate what the body itself produces, which is a built-in apothecary, without the disadvantages of the toxicity of drugs.

Dr. Franz Inglefinger, former editor of the prestigious *New England Journal of Medicine,* stated that 85 percent of all people who bring complaints and symptoms to their physicians suffer from "self-limiting" disorders. This means that more than four times out of five, what ails you is well within the reach of the body's own healing mechanisms. Contrary to popular belief, doctors really don't heal anything; it's always our own internal mechanism that does the healing. The physician merely helps suppress the symptoms by giving you a drug that may alleviate them so that you won't be as aware of your discomfort until your body has a chance to heal itself. But, of course, every drug is toxic and has some side effect; in fact, some drugs are very poisonous. With the exception of bacterial infections such as sexually transmitted diseases, for example, it is always wiser to facilitate healing by natural means, instead of suppressing the symptom by medicating it.

A disease is not merely a physical problem, isolated in the body, but a problem of the whole person. Our emotions play a significant role not only in susceptibility to disease, but in recovery. Illness is usually a symptom of problems elsewhere in an individual's life. Mind and body are one inseparable system; whatever affects the mind affects the body. The converse is also true. Every thought we think, no matter how innocuous, has an immediate physiological effect; everything a person thinks, feels, and believes is experienced directly in the body. If we consciously change our thoughts to those that are healthy, joyful, and loving, we will radiate these feelings within our bodies and can produce the corresponding effect. If we recognize we play a part in creating our own illnesses through our thoughts and emotions, then we can realize that we can play a part in creating our own health, and our mental attitude can promote or obstruct our body's self-healing.

Dr. Lawrence LeShan, clinical psychologist and author of several books on the mind's role in health and disease, including *You Can Fight for Your Life,* writes:

> The mind has untapped potential far beyond the everyday uses that we make of it. Self-healing is a major factor in curing most illnesses. A patient's mental attitude can help or hinder the body's self-healing mechanisms. Through various forms of meditation, the power of the mind or psyche can be enlisted for the purpose of speeding up the healing process.

Some years ago I met Glenda in a Concept-Therapy class. She was a fifty-five-year-old woman whose hands were so crippled with arthritis that she could not dress herself or comb her hair. Six months later, she had completely arrested the arthritis, felt no pain, and her hands were totally mobile. How could this be? Glenda learned the principles of mental healing described in this chapter. She began talking to her hands daily and specifically directing the calcium deposits in the joints of her fingers to break down and be eliminated through her body in a normal fashion. She came to realize that there is *consciousness* in every molecule of matter, even in the abnormal growth in her hands. More importantly, this consciousness can be contracted and directed when we understand its laws, and it will do our bidding when we approach it correctly. At the same time, Glenda began psychotherapy to release the deep-seated resentment she had held for forty years toward her ex-husband, who had been caught with another woman the day after her marriage. Her arthritis began shortly thereafter, and her fingers eventually tightened into a position similar to someone about to strangle a person.

The New Synthesis

In the past decade, there has been a quiet revolution in the medical field resulting in the somewhat hesitant acceptance of alternative methods of healing, including practitioners of acupuncture, hypnosis, naturopathy, relaxation training, homeopathy, chiropractic, and nutritional therapists who recognize the contribution vitamins and minerals can play in health maintenance. Mind control, such as using mental imagery in healing, positive affirmations, and meditation and relaxation techniques, are also being taught to promote well-being.

In the last decade, there has been a synthesis of ancient and modern techniques, such as traditional medicine and metaphysics, Zen Buddhism and quantum physics. The archaic mind/body dualism of Descartes has been replaced by the knowledge that mind and body are unified, and whatever affects a part, affects the whole. When body and mind function together in harmony, health exists. Illness results when stress and conflict disrupt this process. Out of this understanding emerges the freedom of each individual to participate actively in creating and sustaining the health of his or her body.

Healing Through Imagery

Carl Simonton, M.D., and the staff of his California clinic, have realized remarkable success using visual imagery in their treatment program for terminally ill cancer patients, and have described the technique in their excellent book *Getting Well Again*. Dr. Simonton is the director of the Simonton Cancer Center in Pacific Palisades, California. While Simonton was chief radiation oncologist at Travis Air Force Base in California, he used the technique with an aviator whose advanced throat cancer portended certain death. The cancer had reached the size of a peach, and was occluding the openings to the lungs and stomach, and spreading rapidly.

Simonton taught the patient a procedure of deep muscular relaxation through which he could enter the alpha state where the brain waves are slowed down from normal activity, so that he was closer to his subconscious mind. He was then told to visualize his cancer in some way, and to fantasize the malignant cells were being destroyed. The patient began to image his white blood cells (part of the body's immune system) as riders on horseback. They began attacking and destroying the cancer cells. This image was repeated for fifteen minutes, three times a day, and over a period of seven weeks the tumor receded in size, and finally disappeared. At the end of this time the patient's biopsy specimens revealed only normal tissue.

Simonton's technique for assisting cancer patients to heal themselves can be used with slight modification in treating any disease. Here are the basic steps:

1. Get into a comfortable position and relax deeply.

2. For about two minutes, picture a pleasant scene, such as walking through the woods on a summer day, strolling along the beach, or sailing on the bay.

3. Visualize your disease. (It doesn't need to be exact. Most of us are sufficiently in touch with our bodies to produce at least a vague idea of what is happening within it.)

4. Picture your immunity mechanism in some fashion: the white blood cells going in and carrying out the dead, destroyed cells and eliminating them through the urine and bowels. See your white cells as very strong, very aggressive, attacking the cancer cells and destroying them. See the cancer shrinking, the liver and kidneys taking it out of the body with the urine and stool. See yourself beginning to feel better, becoming more in tune with life, having more energy, a better appetite,

more pleasant relationships. Frequently, during the day, affirm:

My body has the ability to repair itself, and it is doing so now!

5. Repeat this procedure three times a day for fifteen minutes each session. If done faithfully and with confidence, at the end of approximately 21 days you will notice a remarkable change!

Mental healing does not, of course, preclude medical assistance. It should be viewed as an adjunct to whatever traditional methods you now use.

One pleasantly warm spring afternoon a few years ago, I received a telephone call from a distraught client who said she had accidentally amputated almost half of her right index finger while trying to repair the chain on an exercise bicycle. She was rushed to a hospital carrying the amputated portion in a saline solution. Initially, the doctor declined to graft the severed piece to the remainder of her finger, stating it was hopeless. Finally, after realizing how distressed Dot was, the physician said he would suture the amputated portion only as a "biological dressing," because the odds of saving the finger were less than a hundred to one. Dot was extremely distressed at the thought of losing her index finger, particularly since she was a computer programmer and spent much of the day typing.

Of all the people I'd counseled, Dot was one of the most decidedly skeptical. A very intelligent, multitalented woman, who relied completely on her intellect to deal with life, at that time she had no awareness of metaphysics or self-healing techniques. Nevertheless, I encouraged her to believe she could heal her finger using the considerable power of her subconscious mind. I instructed her in the techniques of visualization, and she began repeating the following affirmations aloud four times each day:

Every day, my finger is becoming more and more whole.

The graft is taking, and the parts are now joining more firmly and completely.

My finger is becoming healthier and healthier and is healing rapidly.

The nail is being restored through growth of a new healthy one.

Thank you Spirit within every cell of my body, for effecting this healing.

In addition, twice a day for fifteen minutes each time, Dot diligently relaxed completely in a comfortable chair, put herself into a state of self-hypnosis, and visualized her finger totally healed and perfectly normal in every way. She also increased her daily regimen of vitamins, particularly taking large dosages of vitamin C to help strengthen her body's immune system while the healing took place. Dot was also more careful about eating healthy, nutritious foods during this period, and was scrupulous about following her doctor's instructions to keep the wound clean with frequent changes of dressing. She supplemented her doctor's suggestions and her own healing concepts by listening twice a day to a self-healing tape I made especially for her.

Ten days after the suturing, Dot encountered a new doctor in the outpatient clinic who insisted that the amputated portion, which had blackened, was necrotic (dead), and must be removed. She was told that she would not be allowed to leave the hospital until that surgery was performed because of the likelihood of gangrene spreading down her arm. When Dot begged for "just a little more time," two other physicians were consulted. One of them agreed that she could retain the graft a little longer. Six days after this she was again told that the amputated portion was indeed dead. But, at Dot's insistence, the doctor again permitted her to retain the graft. Twenty-six days after the accident, the doctor finally acknowledged that the finger was healing and stated: "I don't know what you're doing, but keep doing it!" At the end of two more months, her finger had completely healed, and appeared perfectly normal.

Healing with Thought

Recently some medical establishments have permitted students in nursing and medical schools to experiment with mental healing as a part of their professional training. "The doors are opening because there is factual evidence for unconventional healing, and you can't argue with facts," says psychologist Evelyn Monahan, who teaches a course on "The Power and Use of the Mind" to students at Emory University's School of Nursing in Atlanta, Georgia. In her course, Dr. Monahan instructs nurses to use telepathy to reach comatose patients, and to use clairvoyance to pick up subliminal leads in analyzing medical histories, plus her specialty, psychic healing. "You can use the mind to affect external things, including the molecular structure of the body," Dr. Monahan believes. One of the most effective techniques is visualization. "I teach the nurses to actually see diseased organs or infections of the body repairing themselves," she explains. "If you want to fight infection, you can visualize the white blood cells speeding to the site of the infection and destroying the invading body."

Dr. Irving Oyle, author of *The Healing Mind,* was an early pioneer in the use of visualization, meditation, and affirmations in self-healing. He states:

> By changing the consciousness, the mental picture you have of what's going on in your body, you can change the physical body, according to this new emerging medical model. By thinking themselves sick, people become sick. We know, for instance, that there is an ulcer-type personality, which is prone to thinking itself into ulcers.

There is a certain type of personality that tends to get heart attacks. If you can think yourself into them, why can't you think yourself out of them? And, if you change the thinking pattern or the visual imagery to restore health, you become your own healer.

The Law of Vibration

Healing yourself or another person comes under one of the natural laws of the universe: the law of vibration. A vibration can be transmitted from one person to another through the medium of the resonant electric waves of the sender's brain cells to the brain cells of the receiver. This has been demonstrated repeatedly through the phenomenon of mental telepathy.

Disease is just a vibration, and so is health; the former being the lower frequency, and health the high. All sickness is nothing but a maladjustment of frequencies, and to effect a healing all we have to do is *change the frequency*. The individual consciousness of the various body organs each have their own frequencies, since all consciousness has its "degree-frequency." Spirit, present within every cell of a patient's body, can be consciously contacted and directed through properly using the law of vibration.

When a drug is given to a sick person, and it helps to effect a healing, all that has happened is that the particular chemical, which vibrates at a certain frequency, has interacted with the patient's frequency to bring it closer to normal. Every drug has its own frequency, which can stimulate the vibration of a patient's organs. Digitalis, for example, is used to stimulate the vibration of the heart, and thereby change its frequency. In the same manner, concentrated thought force can increase, stimulate, and restore the patient's overall frequency to produce a condition of perfectly normal functioning. It's the same principle used in a mental way, but without side effects.

If you change the vibration of something, you change its form, its condition. In order to change a vibration, we must apply energy, and in mental healing, energy in the form of thought. For example, on the physical plane, one can change ice into water by applying energy in the form of heat, and we have actually changed its form by speeding up its vibration. Then we can take that same water and apply energy to it, which means to step up its vibration further, and it will become steam. Here again, by changing the vibration, we have changed the form. We use the same principle in changing disease into health. If you apply energy in the form of your concentrated thought vibrations, you will change the form or condition from one of illness to one of health.

A woman who attended one of my seminars at the University of Santa Clara in California was scheduled for an operation to have a tumor removed from her uterus. When Sandy told me about it, I suggested it would be worthwhile to try imagery first to see if the surgery could be avoided. With Sandy's permission, we organized a healing group of five people and, at separate locations at the designated time of 9 P.M., each one of us spent ten minutes sending healing energy to Sandy, concentrating on seeing her healthy and happy. At the end of twelve days she was reexamined by her doctor, who told her he couldn't find any evidence of the tumor. The operation was postponed indefinitely.

At the same time, another student told me he was to have an operation on his prostate gland and was very concerned about it. That evening I went to a study group meeting where twenty people were present, and asked everyone to join me in an image for Richard's health. Because of the personal nature of the problem, I didn't describe it to the group, but led an image in which we visualized him smiling, healthy, and active. A few days later he was feeling so good that he checked with his doctor again who decided that he could postpone the operation. To this day, he has never had to have it.

Absent Healing

To change a person's vibration on a conscious level, we must first establish a condition of resonance or rapport with that person for our suggestion to lodge in his or her subconscious mind. When two minds are in harmony, mental telepathy, or the transmission of thought, is possible. Do not attempt to give a healing suggestion to someone who will scoff at you, because the suggestion will not penetrate their subconscious mind. In such cases, send them healing thoughts when you're away from them, because this bypasses the conscious mind.

Absent healing, either with a group or alone, can be very effective. The following is a technique you can use whenever necessary (see "A Healing Image," page 157). Of course, if an individual has become ill through repeated indulgence in negative emotions, such as anger, depression, or fear, then mental healing will only be effective for a limited period of time, for the simple reason that the person will once again make himself "diseased" through disturbed emotions. The same thing applies, of course, to traditional medical means of healing; the cure is only temporary if the individual doesn't change his or her lifestyle and thinking process. Either the illness will reappear, or symptom substitution will occur. Healing is a matter of the entire psyche, not just the physical body.

In conditions of semiconsciousness, or unconsciousness, the suggestions should be given aloud because they will be directly received by the subconscious. When people are in a coma, under anesthesia, in a state of shock after an accident, having a seizure, or sleeping, their subconscious minds are wide open. Anything that is said in their presence will be accepted by Spirit, which will begin carrying it out. In these cases you contact Spirit directly, without intervention from the conscious reasoning mind, and it's always Spirit that does the healing, no matter the method—pill, shot, surgery, chiropractic adjustment, traction, or whatever. Always remember that *you* have no power to heal, but you can be an instrument for Spirit to affect a change in the body of the afflicted person. All you have to do to help someone is to give positive, constructive healing concepts to Spirit, and it will do the work. Remember, the Power that made the body can heal the body!

An additional mental healing technique, used down through the ages by psychics and spiritual healers, is to visualize a beautiful white light cascading over the head, shoulders, and body of the afflicted individual. See this pure, brilliant healing light penetrating deeply into every cell and pore of the body, cleansing and purifying it, and bringing the body up to a level of perfectly normal functioning. This is an effective technique for all mental healing, and it is said by metaphysicians that a "thought form" is actually created around the person on the astral plane.

The primary fact we must become increasingly aware of is that thoughts and mental images can initiate *physiological changes in our bodies*. We can learn to control our thoughts and direct positive energy to ourselves and others, and thus become an active participant in creating and maintaining our own health. Remember, thought is creative, and your own thinking processes can bring you perfect health, energy, and stamina.

Dr. Fleet says:

> Man must take responsibility for the state of his body, for we are the product of our thought creations. Whatever condition our body is in, and whatever the state of our mind, is a replication of what we have selected from the thought plane, manifesting in our life. Every illness in your or my body is a direct result of some image in our mental life.
>
> When a person knows this, and properly understands it, he or she will naturally begin to image correctly. Instead of violating this Law of Creation and worrying

about the things one does not want, people will begin to visualize and image and fashion and plan that which they do want, and we will have a new world, and all of our disease-ridden bodies will be replaced by healthy ones.

A Healing Image

1. Prearrange with the sick person and with others who have agreed to participate, the time you are going to make your image. (8 P.M. is preferable.)

2. A few moments before the designated time, go into a room where you will be alone for ten minutes, turn out the lights, seat yourself in a comfortable chair, relax yourself, and begin to *visualize* the sick person sitting in his or her chair or bed, in a passive, receptive state of mind. Their own Creative Power Within is as open as possible to receive the curative image.

3. As you picture this person, say the following aloud:

   Spirit Within is healing you now.

   Every day, in every way,

   You are becoming healthier and healthier.

4. Repeat this over and over, in a singsong tone of voice. Do not use your will, but use your imagination when you repeat the affirmation, and strongly *visualize* the person looking and acting completely healthy in every way.

5. Feel that the person's subconscious mind is receiving your message and concentrate as much as possible on sending your positive thoughts to them. Imagine that the person is surrounded by a white healing light pouring down and throughout their entire body, penetrating deeply into every cell, organ, nerve, and muscle, bringing the entire vibration of their body up to a

state of *perfectly normal functioning*, whatever is normal for that particular individual. *See* this light penetrating deeply into their body and see the person smiling, healthy, and happy.

6. At the end of ten minutes, turn the image over to Spirit to carry it out in the person's body. Then, break your concentration and leave the room.

Do not try to reach the subconscious mind unless you put your heart into this. Put all your concentration into the idea of "Perfect Health," and try not to think of anything else while you are in the room. Spirit will receive your message and act upon it, and the sick person will be forever grateful to you for using your helpful energies. The Law of Cause and Effect will then operate in *your* life to keep you in perfect health.

Everything depends on one's opinion. We suffer
according to our opinion. One is as miserable or
as happy as one believes oneself to be.

SENECA

TEN
How to Stay
Healthy All Your Life

Although this book deals
with cognitive methods to improve our lives, we
must not overlook the importance of keeping our
bodies healthy. Physical health is probably one of the
most important things in the world, because without
it our lives are constricted and impoverished.

The good news is that there really are methods to
ensure you will be a healthy person your entire life,
and need not end up a sick, crippled invalid in a nursing home, being pushed in a wheelchair. It is a myth,
which is increasingly becoming disproved, that old age
must mean incapacity, senility, and a host of degenera-
tive diseases. We are very fortunate to live in a time
when science and alternative health practitioners are
discovering methods of prevention and self-healing

that cannot only prolong your life, but allow you to enjoy your golden years free from the so-called "diseases of old age." You may not be aware of how much you can do to slow down, or even reverse, the changes that usually accompany aging. It will take some work on your part to bring about this happy ending. No matter how young or old you may be, *now* is the time to start.

According to what we now know about good health, here are the seven ingredients for staying healthy all your life:

1. Stress reduction: proper thinking and expression of feelings.

2. Regular exercise.

3. Proper nutrition.

4. Adequate rest and relaxation.

5. No substance abuse (drugs/alcohol/smoking).

6. Social contact: love/family/friends/pets.

7. Take as few drugs as possible, prescribed or over-the-counter.

The Mind/Body Connection

The new medical model recognizes the mind as a factor in every disease, except perhaps the very few diseases and illnesses caused by external agents, such as poisons. Dr. Kenneth Pelletier, author of *Mind as Healer, Mind as Slayer,* believes that all illnesses are in some way psychosomatic; not in the sense that they're imaginary, but in the sense that they all involve mental and physical factors.

Andrew Weil, M.D., author of *Eight Weeks to Optimal Health,* states that: "Agents of disease are not the causes of disease. The underlying causes of disease are *internal.* . . . All illness is psychosomatic. The mind and body are interdependent and together can cause or prevent sickness." Stated at its simplest, the conclusion is: our health is controlled by our brain. The intimate connection between the state of the mind and the state of the body has finally gained acceptability. In scientific circles the study of this field even has a fancy new name: *Psychoneuroimmunology.* There is a professional journal by the same name, but the concept is based on a very old idea. It has been known for centuries that a person's psychological state can affect his or her health, but science is finally discovering how this occurs. This is leading to new ways to treat disease, particularly the methods now used by holistic health practitioners—those who treat the whole person, not just the body.

Emotions as a Factor in Disease

Aided by new biochemical techniques and a vastly expanded understanding of neurochemistry and immunology, new studies prove that our emotions affect our nervous system, glandular system (hormonal levels, adrenaline production, etc.), and the response of our immune system—all of which affect our susceptibility to a host of illnesses. Studies have revealed that emotional reactions can suppress or stimulate disease-fighting white blood cells and trigger the release of adrenal gland hormones and endorphins, morphine-like chemicals produced by the neurotransmitters of the brain, that in turn affect dozens of bodily processes. It is becoming increasingly accepted that emotions are *necessary components* of the cause, as well as the treatment, of most illnesses. The new studies show that virtually every physical problem—from the common cold to cancer and coronary disease—can be influenced, positively or negatively, by a person's mental state. Researchers speculate that chronic indulgence in negative emotions creates a lowered resistance to disease by interfering with the ability of the immune system to fight back.

Today, there is a great deal of talk about the connection between stress and disease—but what exactly is stress? Basically, stress is comprised of negative emotions, such as worry, anxiety, depression, feelings of hostility, guilt, anger, and so forth. A commuter stuck for hours in traffic can generate a lot of frustration and anger, which swirls throughout his body. If you're suddenly cut off by a speeding car, you are startled and scared, and then angry. Having your loan for that perfect house fall through because of a mistake on your credit report can create a host of emotions, all of them negative. Worry about who will care for your aging parents can cause your shoulders to droop. Fear creates stress, and anxiety causes muscles to contract and blood vessels to constrict. When blood can't be transported freely through the body to provide oxygen, nutrients, and antibodies, and to carry away and dispose of toxic waste materials, illness sets in.

Personality Factors Related to Certain Diseases

Diseases are not haphazard; they don't just come out of the blue and strike a person one fine day without any antecedents. Current research demonstrates that, if you are prone to getting a disease, the type you contract will be something specifically related to your personality, a theory called "psychosomatic specificity."

This is because different emotions act on different parts of the body and produce differing chemical reactions, resulting in specific types of diseases. Every thought produces a physiological effect. The effects they produce are chemical substances such as adrenaline and ACTH. When your thoughts produce chemicals such as these at the wrong time, or in excessive amounts, the result is an impaired immune system.

Coronary Personality

Much has been written, for example, about the type of person most prone to coronary disease, the Type A personality—hard-driving, impatient, hostile, demanding of himself and others, highly competitive, and usually involved in multiple projects. "Cynicism, better than any other word, captures the toxic element in the Type A personality," says Redford Williams of Duke University Medical Center. "If a more trusting attitude can be learned, help for heart patients may be on the way." Williams and his colleagues did a series of experiments to determine this.

According to psychological tests, the "hostility" scores of Type A people were significantly higher than those of Type B. High scorers were 50 percent more likely to have coronary artery blockages than were low scorers. After analyzing the responses of 1,500 people to fifty items, Williams found a concise unifying theme: cynicism, a contemptuous distrust of human nature and motives.* When we are frequently hostile, excessive secretion of norepinephrene, a brain chemical, contributes to our risk of hypertension, arteriosclerosis, or heart attack.

Cancer Personality

In his book *You Can Fight for Your Life,* Dr. Lawrence LeShan identified four typical components in the life histories of the more than 500 cancer patients with whom he worked. One component was that the patient's youth was marked by feelings of isolation, neglect, and despair, and close interpersonal relationships seemed difficult and dangerous.

Second, in early adulthood, the patient was able to establish a strong, meaningful relationship with a person, or found great satisfaction in his or her vocation. A tremendous amount of energy was poured into this relationship or role. Indeed, it became the reason for living, the center of the patient's life. The relationship or role was then removed—through death, divorce, a move, a child leaving home, job loss, or the like, and the patient was unable to find a substitute. The result was despair, as though the "wound" left over from childhood had been painfully reopened.

One of the fundamental characteristics of these patients was that the despair was bottled up. They were unable to let other people know when they felt hurt, angry, or sad. Others frequently

---

* Williams, Jr., R. B., et al. (1980). "Type A Behavior, hostility, and coronary atherosclerosis." *Psychosomatic Medicine,* 42(6), 539–549.

viewed the cancer patients as unusually wonderful people, saying such things as: "He's such a good, sweet man" or "She's a saint." LeShan concludes: "The benign quality, the 'goodness' of these people was in fact a sign of their failure to believe in themselves sufficiently, and of their lack of hope."

A client of mine who died of colon cancer typified this personality type. Loretta had four children and had never worked outside the home. That is, she had never done work for which she was paid, but after her children had grown, she devoted herself to volunteer work and spent endless hours helping others. Until she came for therapy, she had never admitted to herself that she didn't feel appreciated, and sometimes even felt used, as she constantly allowed others to take advantage of her. Incredibly, she even felt guilty whenever she did something solely for herself, instead of taking care of others. This fifty-eight-year-old woman didn't believe she deserved to have a life of her own and her low self-esteem contributed to her death.

Keep in mind that not all of the characteristics LeShan describes apply to every cancer patient. Another element of his description, that cancer patients tend to be prone to feelings of hopelessness and helplessness before the onset of their disease, has been confirmed by other studies. Considerable evidence has shown that the immune system is impaired in people who feel unable to cope with adversity, and a feeling of helplessness may be a key factor in vulnerability to cancer. When we feel depressed and helpless for extended periods, the chemicals our body releases suppress the ability of the immune surveillance system to screen out cells that lead to cancer.

Dr. Carl Simonton and his partner, Stephanie Matthews-Atchley, specialized in working with cancer patients for a number of years using traditional methods, plus guided imagery. Together with James Creighton, they wrote an excellent book, *Getting Well Again,* a step-by-step guide to overcoming cancer for patients and their families. In the book, Dr. Simonton reports that, almost always, the cancer is triggered by the loss of a serious love object, occurring one year to eighteen months prior to the diagnosis in people who have suffered a loss early in their lives. Usually there is a major loss, such as a job, a death, or divorce, followed by deep feelings of sadness, anxiety, and hopelessness. When there also has been an early childhood loss, this later loss triggers the feelings of hopelessness that accompanied the first one.

There is now confirmed evidence that grief, loneliness, helplessness, and negative attitudes like anger and fear can measurably depress immune system functioning. Antibody production, thymus function, and the activity of T and B helper cells are all weakened by negative thoughts. When we feel our problems are beyond our control, the hormone cortisol increases, making us more vulnerable to infections. Even Louis Pasteur, who gained prominence in the late nineteenth century for his discovery of germs, recognized that the host (the person) had to be in a certain state of debility before germs could settle into the body. He spoke of the disease process being dependent on the underlying health of the body to begin with.

People with strong needs to dominate have depressed immune defenses when they face certain stressful situations. The person with hypertension, for example, may believe he must constantly be ready for battle, so his body behaves as though it were going to be attacked and keeps his blood pressure high. Hypertensive people are often exactly as the term implies: overreactors and overresponders. Hypertension is more likely to occur in persons who feel as though they must always be ready for combat with some outside source, although their aggression is usually held in check.

When we feel we're in danger (such as anticipating a fight with our boss or partner), our heart rate speeds up, the fats, cholesterol, and sugar in our blood stream increases, our stomach secretes more acid, and our immune system slows down. All of these sudden changes are an enormous strain on our system. Over time, this pressure leads to symptoms such as gastrointestinal distress, high cholesterol levels, insomnia, headaches, and back pain. It also leaves us more vulnerable to infections.

We can easily see the direct relationship of our emotions upon our bodily functions when we experience strong feelings such as fear and anger. Suppose, for example, you are in a scary situation, such as giving a speech before a large group of people, or a presentation to the boss and your coworkers. Your brain is given the message: "I'm threatened in this situation." This message goes directly to the autonomic nervous system (ANS), the involuntary system that controls your heartbeat, breathing, digestion, and other internal activities. The ANS automatically responds to the brain's message of threat by producing more adrenaline, speeding up your heartbeat, activating the sweat glands, reducing saliva, tightening the stomach muscles, and increasing the activities of all the other bodily processes that accompany fear, temporarily throwing your entire system out of order.

Instead of fear, let's suppose you become very angry at your boss. Your brain sends this stress message to the ANS, and the internal organs are immediately activated to war production. Blood is driven out of the abdominal cavity to the lungs, the muscles, and the brain, bringing them their needed increase of energy for action. Your blood pressure rises. Carbohydrates are moved out of storage in the liver and muscles and converted into fuel for action. The adrenal glands, which are the fighting glands, pour their stimulating hormones into your bloodstream, your muscles tighten, and your entire body is made ready for flight or fight.

Primitive man would have done one or the other, but modern man can usually do neither. Instead, he puts a smile on his face and tries not to reveal his true feelings. Naturally, this whole procedure puts the body under tremendous stress and interrupts the body's homeostasis, making it more vulnerable to disease. If this indulgence in anger occurs repeatedly, the constant rise in blood pressure may lead to hypertension, or possibly a stroke, or the chronic muscular tension can cause arthritis or toxic thyroidism. The disturbance in carbohydrate metabolism may eventually produce diabetes, or any of a number of other diseases may begin to manifest.

Suffice to say that when a person indulges in strong, negative emotions, such as fear, anger, chronic depression, jealousy, worry, or thoughts of revenge, every system in the body becomes disturbed. If this is repeated long enough, the organism will eventually break down. That is the major cause of disease.

The primary premise of the medical model that we have all been programmed to for several centuries is that germs are the cause of disease. Although germs certainly contribute to illness, there is *no single cause* for disease. Rather, *disease is multifactored* and is the result of a number of things a person does as they go about their life. Because of this, disease is ultimately under the control of the person, and not some haphazard thing. It's the choices we make as we travel down the highway of life that makes the difference between a healthy or unhealthy body. Disease is not some unfortunate contact with a single evil agent, such as a germ or virus that is lurking everywhere and may suddenly spring on us. The traditional medical establishment propagates the idea of evil germs, or of bad luck—it just happened without any antecedent cause, and you're the victim. The doctor, of course, is the savior, who we hope will fix us with either drugs or surgery. Lacking some genetic cause, the power to stay healthy remains within each individual, and our everyday choices will determine the outcome. Healing doesn't rest in the hands of a select few, but in each human being. No matter what physicians or drugs do, they can only enhance the healing process of the body itself.

Tuberculosis Personality

In his remarkable, well-researched book *Who Gets Sick: Thinking and Health,* Dr. Blair Justice states:

Although the presence of the tubercle bacillus is a necessary condition for tuberculosis, other factors must be present for the disease to occur. Control of the bacteria has proved difficult as demonstrated by the fact that the majority of adults today are tuberculin positive—are infected—although most never show clinical signs of the disease. In fact, for every 100 Caucasian Americans now becoming infected with the tubercle bacillus, 99 percent do not develop the classic pulmonary disease. In the midst of his pioneering study on stress, Dr. Hans Selye observed that reactions to psychological threats could trigger a person's latent tubercle bacilli. He noted the importance that rest—freedom from stress—continued to play in the treatment of disease.

Herpes and Stress

Many people carry the herpes simplex virus that erupts in cold sores. It is now known that psychological stress can precipitate outbreaks of this normally latent Type 1 herpes virus. Researchers from the University of Pennsylvania found that students who were frequently unhappy had a higher incidence of cold sore episodes during the year. The greatest effects were found among students with high loneliness scores and those who were depressed. Students facing exams have also been reported to have an increased incidence of cold sores.†

Psychiatrist Janie Kiecolt-Glaser of Ohio State reported that over-stressed medical students studying for important exams showed poorer immune function than they did during summer vacations. In another study this psychiatrist reported in the journal *Psychosomatic Medicine,* that medical students had decreases in helper T-cells on the day of exams. But, when half the group were taught relaxation exercises, their T-cells increased. The percent of

---

† Luborsky, L., et al. (1976). "Herpes simplex virus and moods: A longitudinal study." *Journal of Psychosomatic Research,* 20 (9).

their disease-fighting T-cells could be predicted by how frequently the students practiced relaxation! ‡

Disease is Multifactored

In *Who Gets Sick*, Dr. Justice states:

> Although heart disease and all other leading causes of death and disability today require the presence of *multiple risk factors*, there is still mounting pressure to explain the appearance of most chronic diseases on the basis of such single variables as cigarette smoking, alcohol consumption, or exposure to other hazardous substances. These substances by themselves do not "cause" disease, although this assumption is widely held despite the fact that the majority of those thus exposed do not succumb prematurely to the disorder in question.

Whether the disease is cancer, coronary problems, or diabetes, it appears that "cofactors," not single causes, are responsible. Cigarettes alone will not cause cancer or heart attacks, but cigarettes, plus other abuses may, because our risk is increased by introducing this toxic substance into the body. But a *key* cofactor in all illness, which is now the subject of intense research by the new science of biological and molecular psychology, is our thinking: how our emotions affect our health and can contribute to making us sick. Since we now know that the brain regulates all bodily functions, including the all-important immune system, our thinking processes are being increasingly implicated as one of the most important contributing factors in the creation of disease.

In *Health and Healing*, Dr. Andrew Weil writes:

---

‡ Kiecolt-Glaser, J. K., et al. (1984). "Psychosocial modifiers of immunocompetence in medical students." *Psychosomatic Medicine*, 46(1) 7–14.

> This point must be stressed: external, material objects are never causes of disease, they are merely agents waiting to cause specific symptoms in susceptible hosts. Rather than making war on disease agents with the hope (in vain, I suspect) of eliminating them, we ought to be more concerned with strengthening our resistance to them. Illness, it seems, occurs more from our general vulnerability, than from external agents.

Since disease is not so much the effect of toxic, external forces or the germs in the air or in our bodies, why do some people get sick and others don't when they are exposed to the same agents? What decides whether a person is at risk of acquiring a particular disease, and under what circumstances will a person develop a disease? Our susceptibility to disease has now been convincingly linked to the way we cope with life; that means how we view the events and situations that occur everyday. The way we react to the daily stresses of life is the *central determinant* of whether or not we will contract a disease. If we have poor coping skills, high stress, poor nutrition, lack exercise, and chronically indulge in negative thinking, then the internal balance of our bodies is easily upset and we are less resistant to disease. The way we react to what Freud called "the psychopathology of everyday life" can determine whether we will get an infection, or remain symptom-free. Since most of the microbes that afflict human beings are already present in our bodies, they will erupt into disease *only* when other risk factors lower our immunity.

Of course we cannot control the world, but we can control our response to it. How does it affect a person's health if they wake up each morning dreading to go to the office? Or dreading to come home at the end of the day? What does it do to the immune system to continue in a job or relationship we hate? J. I. Rodale, founder of *Prevention* magazine, published a book in 1970 with the interesting title: *Happy People Rarely Get Cancer.* On the other hand, the unhappy person is the target for any kind of illness.

Three personality factors that make us prone to disease were identified in a very informative book *The Complete Guide to Your Emotions and Your Health* by Emrika Padus and the editors of *Prevention* magazine. They are:

1. **Control.** How much we believe we need to control is a key determinant of how distressed we will be if we appraise a situation as being beyond our control. Some people have high needs for power, that is, they must not only control the situation, but impress and influence others.

2. **Need for Approval.** Some people have strong affiliative needs; they want to be loved and accepted by everyone, and they are always seeking approval, and become depressed when they don't get it.

3. **Perfectionism.** A third group is made up of those who need to perform perfectly in whatever they do, and of course they're doomed to failure because nobody can be perfect.

We all have to face a great many crises, and sometimes even very severe trauma, in the course of living a life. But, it seems it's not so much the number or severity of the stresses in life that create illness, but how we react to them. Far more important is the interpretation we give to the situation and our resultant response. Dr. Hans Selye, author of *The Stress of Life,* an endocrinologist who was one of the world's foremost researchers on stress, came to the conclusion that it is not the stress per se, of a particular situation that impacts us, but how we appraise that situation.

Going with the Flow

What predisposes us to disease is not the difficulties of our lives, but how we cope with our difficulties. For example, suppose you're driving down the freeway and someone passes you giving you a rude gesture. If you just drive on and let the incident go by thinking: "It's too bad some people are so uptight today that every little thing elicits a hostile response," you're not likely to experience any physiological consequences of any significance. However, if you choose to fight back by doing the same to him, or employ some other angry response (besides risking being attacked), your entire nervous system will become alarmed and tense and you will discharge adrenaline that increases your blood pressure in anticipation of combat. If you happen to be a coronary candidate, the result could be a heart attack. The question then would be: What caused your death? The driver? His insult? No, you caused your own death by allowing yourself to become tense and angry by someone else's actions.

According to Dr. Albert Ellis, psychologist and author of A Guide to Rational Living, emotions have very little to do with actual events. In between the event and emotion is a realistic, or unrealistic, assessment of it through our inner dialogue, and it is our self-talk that produces the emotions. Our own thoughts, directed and controlled by us alone, are what cause anxiety, anger, guilt, tension, depression, or hostility, or in a word, stress. We assume that things are done to us, such as "She makes me angry . . . being lied to makes me see red . . . the boss makes me nervous . . . people talking like that depresses me," etc. But these things are not actually done to us: we choose our own reaction through our interpretation of the situation and our consequent self-talk. The way out is through self-awareness. Tune into your body. If you become aware that reacting negatively to the daily hassles of life is creating tension, fatigue, headaches, backache, heartburn, and so forth, you might want to reexamine your responses and learn to become more tolerant toward others' inappropriate behavior. When people change how they look at problems, and see them as challenges, or simply temporary setbacks, and understand that they can at least control how they react to them, this helps restore and maintain a proper biochemical balance in the body.

Our reactions are determined by our basic beliefs and perceptions. Learning to control our thinking means learning how to appraise difficult situations so we can reduce their impact on our nervous system. To do this we must be aware of our own internal dialogue, and try to respond to events as positively as possible. Thinking about events negatively, or acting evasively in order not to have to deal with them, sets us up for illness. *Attitude is everything!*

According to studies reported in *The Complete Guide to Your Emotions and Your Health,* the personality traits that help people confront stress the most are the "3 C's": Commitment, Control, and Challenge. These traits add up to what psychologists call "hardiness." It's the hardy people who survive longest and are the most resistant to illness.

1. *Commitment* to work, family, self-improvement, and other important values.

2. A sense of personal *Control* over one's life.

3. The ability to see change and stressful events in one's life as a *Challenge* to master.

People who are able to act decisively and positively toward the daily challenges of living are the ones who beat illness, whether it's cancer or coronary disease. Their positive thinking and enthusiasm induce T-cells and other lymphocytes to increase in number to devour malignant cells and other germs. In such people, the daily hassles such as traffic congestion, breaking a favorite vase, or spilling the wine while having dinner with the boss, are simply minor problems in the ongoing drama of life; they refuse to be upset about them. They know, for instance, that while waiting for the traffic to move, they can either lean back and enjoy some good music, or an educational audiotape, and get home feeling relaxed and having benefited from the time alone in which they can unwind, or they can become tense and angry at the situation, and arrive home *at exactly the same time* with elevated blood pressure and pulse rate, ready for a fight. You can play it either way—and you get to choose! As clinical researcher Stewart Wolf, M.D., has said: "Disease is a way of life, it is the end result of the way that people react to life's problems."

Talking Back to the Television

We should also mention here the power negative suggestions from others have to adversely affect our health. We are continually bombarded through our advertising media with suggestions that we will get this or that illness, and we must become aware of the subtle influence these concepts have on our subconscious mind, and learn how to counteract them. We are assaulted on a daily basis through television, magazines, newspapers, etc., with suggestions that it's "cold season"; the flu is going around; do you have a headache? Arthritis? Sinusitis? Stomach ache? Constipation? Heartburn? and so forth. Our brain cells are kept in a state of constant vibration concerning these illnesses. These continual negative suggestions become lodged in our subconscious mind and, if repeated frequently enough, increase our stress, lower our resistance, and can actually contribute to setting us up for disease.

The answer is to become consciously aware of this type of brainwashing and set up a counterresponse to such negative suggestions. Wouldn't it be wonderful if we turned on our television and heard the announcer say: "Nine out of ten doctors recommend relaxation training, meditation, taking a day off for mental health, or just giving someone a hug as a remedy for headaches, backaches, arthritis, and other ailments." Unfortunately, no one would sponsor such an announcement; there's no money in it. Harboring in our mind constant fears of major health catastrophes such as cancer or heart attacks, can help attract these diseases to us. Instead, use the principles of imagery and positive affirmations, and concentrate on ideas that are health- and vitality-oriented.

In the final analysis, all disease comes down to one thing: we have impeded the flow of energy through our bodies. Why? Because we are afraid. Fear is the fundamental emotion and the basis of all our negative emotions. We are afraid to be vulnerable, afraid to be hurt, afraid we might appear stupid, afraid we'll be rejected by someone, and afraid to reveal who we really are because we're afraid of criticism. With all of this holding back, the constant defending, constant distrust, constant "shoulds," we stop the proper flow of our vital energy, and set ourselves up for disease. In health or disease, again, attitude is everything!

The Healing Power of Love

Love is good for your health! Research has shown that lovers get fewer colds because the germ-fighting white blood cells perform better when a person is in love. Being in love also makes your lactic acid level drop so you have more energy. Everyone knows lovers can get by on very little sleep; your body feels more energetic, and there's a bounce to your step when there's romance on your mind.

Of course, it's not always possible to be in love, and some people don't have a partner. But love isn't limited to one's mate. There are many avenues and opportunities to give and receive love. If you don't have anyone in your life right now to give you love, then you must begin by giving it to someone else, and the law of cause and effect ensures that it will come back to you. Extending one's self into the community in some way, and giving love to others is a necessary ingredient for health; it is medicine for the soul and body. Almost any kind of loving relationship can contribute to good health, including love for our pets. For those who don't have a partner, family, or pets, getting involved in a group and helping achieve the group's goals establishes social bonds and prevents us from focusing solely on ourselves. Isolated people are more susceptible to illness.

Dr. Scott Peck, in *The Road Less Traveled,* gives an excellent definition of love:

> Love is the will to extend one's self for the purpose of nurturing one's own or another's spiritual growth. When we grow as persons we need to work at it, and we work at it because we love ourselves and want to improve and elevate ourselves. And it is through our love for others that we want to assist them to elevate themselves. Love, the extension of the self, is the highest act of evolution. It is evolution in progress. The evolutionary force, present in all of life, manifests itself in mankind as human love. Among humanity love is the miraculous force that helps and heals and elevates all of life.

Love and friendship are great stress reducers. When we know we have people we can turn to in trying times, we feel stronger, more confident, less isolated, and more in control of situations. Knowing we have supportive people in our lives, whether it's our mate, our family, or our friends, provides a feeling of security and hope, which helps reduce stress. Sociability of any kind is worth cultivating for the sake of our mental and physical health. Limited and restricted expression of affection and tenderness toward others almost guarantees a compromised immune system. Mounting evidence is showing that people who belong to a network of community, and have friends and relatives are happier, healthier, better able to cope with life, and remarkably resistant to emotional and physical ills.

The Healing Power of Touch

Research now confirms what psychologists have been saying for years: being touched in an affectionate way is vital to our well-being. Dr. James Hardison, psychologist and author of *Let's Touch,* says: "It is through touching that we are able to fulfill a large share of our human needs and, in doing so, to attain happiness. By touching someone we can affirm our friendship or approval, communicate important messages, promote health and bring about love." The problem is we have been trained to put up a lot of barriers to being touched. "For one thing," says Dr. Hardison, "our society tends to equate touching with either sex or violence. Consequently, many people avoid the simple acts of touching—pats on the back, heartfelt handshakes, cordial hugs— that affirm goodwill."

Our lives would be barren and impoverished without the kind of touching that implies real caring. Touch is a means of communication so crucial that its absence retards growth in infants, and it has direct and important effects on the growth of the body as well as the mind. Researchers have found that premature infants gain weight faster and leave the hospital sooner if their mothers touch, rock, and talk to them. A study done at Rush-Presbyterian-St. Luke's Medical Center in Chicago showed that babies touched at regular intervals by their mothers left the hospital an average of four days earlier than normal. The massaged infants also showed signs that their nervous systems were maturing more rapidly; they became more active than the other babies and were more responsive to such things as a face or a rattle. They also gained more weight, although they did not eat more than the others, and this seemed to be due to the effect of contact on their metabolism. The new research suggests that certain brain chemicals released by touch may account for these results. Studies by Dr. Theodore Wacks, a psychologist at Purdue University, showed that infants who experienced more skin-to-skin contact had an advantage in mental development in the first six months of life.

Reaching out to touch other human beings in a caring fashion should be a part of our everyday lives. For those who live alone, and may also work in environments where touching others is inappropriate, loving and nurturing a pet can provide the same fulfillment. Pets offer us love no matter what. Lacking that, there are organizations available to everyone (or volunteer work) where we can share friendly touching companionship—it's medicine for our soul!

Eat to Live, Not Live to Eat

Hippocrates once said: "Let your food be your medicine; let your medicine be your food."

Another important component in maintaining good health is proper nutrition. In 1997, in the first sweeping report on diet and cancer since the 1980s, medical experts from around the world concluded that 30 to 40 percent of all cancers could be avoided just by changing lifestyles and eating habits. They recommended a vegetarian-based diet, no smoking or drinking, and regular exercise. The report, sponsored by the American Institute for Cancer Research and the World Cancer Research states: "If eaten at all, limit intake of red meat to less than three ounces daily. It is preferable to choose fish, poultry and other meat in place of red meat, and have five servings of fruits and vegetables every day."

Unfortunately, in this technological, over-populated, over-polluted, over-"chemicalized" society, we can't get all the nutrients we need from food alone. Much of the food we buy today goes through approximately forty different processes before we actually eat it, and each process reduces its nutritional value. U.S. regulatory agencies allow over 3,000 different chemicals to be added to our foods, and the average American consumes *five pounds* of these toxic chemicals every year, and all of these synthetic products stress the immune system. The Food and Drug Administration and some doctors, have pronounced that practically no one needs diet supplementation if they just eat a balanced diet. Few biochemists and other health professionals who have really studied nutrition believe this potentially dangerous assertion. The chances are the doctors who declare this are not very healthy themselves. Dr. Carlton Fredericks, a renowned nutritionist and author of many books on the subject, says: "The person free of disease is abnormal in our society." The United States is the sickest nation on earth; believe it or not, we come in 93rd place, according to a study reported in *Prevention* magazine. Yet we have more doctors than any other nation.

Vitamins and Your Health

If you want to "just get by" with your health, then don't take vitamins. If, however, you would like to be in optimum health, then it is absolutely necessary that you take supplements every day. Dr. Fox, creator of the Fox diet, says: "I give all my patients a vitamin analysis and dietary survey. I have yet to find a patient with the proper amount and balance of vitamins and nutrients."

Vitamins enhance the body's natural ability to restore and maintain its health. We could not live without vitamins, because they are enormously important in keeping the body well. They are a nutritional necessity because they act to protect us from pollutants in the atmosphere, chemicals in our food and in the clothes we put on our bodies. Pesticides and herbicides in our food can actually do physical damage to our cells, such as hardening the arteries by injuring the blood vessel walls. Vitamin protection actually neutralizes these chemicals and helps eliminate them from the body. They also neutralize specific brain toxins that build up and interfere with normal brain activity, thereby improving brain function.

If it were possible to live in an environment where the soil was free of chemicals and had not been stripped of its nutrients, and the air we breathe were uncontaminated by poisons, then we would not need supplementary vitamins; but this is decidedly not the case. Synthetic hormones and growth regulators are regularly injected into foods, and deplete them of their natural vitamins. Much of the nutritive value of many foods is destroyed before we even buy it. It's grown in soil depleted of minerals, force grown with high-nitrogen fertilizers, genetically altered and sprayed with pesticides. We may feel we get our daily quota of vitamin C when we eat an orange or grapefruit, but this is not necessarily so. The fruit has usually been injected with chemicals to preserve it and give it a nicer color, and it's been sprayed with insecticides. All of this depletes the vitamins and minerals that our bodies need to counteract the effect of poisonous chemcials. Additionally, essential nutrients are destroyed in processed foods, and other nutrients deteriorate during shipping and storage. Yet we are deluded into thinking if we just eat properly, we'll get all the vitamins and minerals we need. In our technological society, this is no longer possible.

Check out the latest U.S. Department of Agriculture food tables on the Internet (www.USDA.gov). After comparing the 1975 version of the tables, researcher Alex Jack discovered that the nutrient value of many foods has dropped dramatically. The vitamin A in apples has gone from 90 mgs to 53 mgs. The amount of vitamin C in red peppers has plummeted from 128 mgs to 89 mgs. There has been a 505 mg drop in the amount of calicum and vitamin A in broccoli, and cauliflower is down 405 mg in vitamin C, B1 and B2. Most of the calcium in pineapple is gone—from 17 mgs (per 100 grams, raw) in 1975 to 7 mgs currently. And the list goes on.§

Vegetables are a major source of vitamins, minerals and phytonutrients, which are absolutely essential to staying healthy. But Americans don't eat enough of them; our favorite foods are bread, doughnuts, pasta, beef, cheese, and pizza. This raises a big question. If people aren't eating their vegetables, and those who do are getting less than they need from them, how are they getting their vitamins? The answer is they're not.

Additionally, some of our lifestyle habits, such as overindulging in coffee, cigarettes, soft drinks or alcohol, burn up or flush out

§ *Life Extension* magazine, 2, 2001.

large amounts of vitamins and minerals. Along with excessive sugar, too much coffee seriously depletes the body's stores of thiamine (vitamin B1). The result is jittery nerves, irritability, and a feeling of being out of control. White sugar, white bread, and other refined foods are deficient in minerals and B vitamins. Sugar also robs our body of essential nutrients in the process of being metabolized, so eating any refined food creates a need for extra B vitamins. Sugar also depletes our body's supply of calcium. Experiments have also shown that refined sugar (which is sucrose) depresses the immune system. That in turn impairs the body's ability to fight infection. Some of the symptoms of this deficient nutrition are the symptoms people experience on a daily basis: headaches, insomnia, fatigue, and irritability.

Drugs also increase the body's need for vitamins and minerals. Medications such as aspirin and other anti-inflammatories greatly increase the body's need for vitamin C. All drugs put additional stress on the body, and thereby increase the need for antistress vitamins such as B-complex. Antibiotics alter normal intestinal bacteria. Problems that can occur as a result are decreased intestinal utilization of a variety of nutrients, including calcium, magnesium, folic acid, and vitamin B12.

Stress also steals our nutrients. Anxiety, anger, and every other kind of stress overtaxes the adrenal glands and robs the body of essential vitamins. "Stress causes a skyrocketing of nutritional needs," says Arthur C. Hochberg, Ph.D., a nutrition-oriented psychologist in Bala Cynwyd, Pennsylvania. One of the B vitamins in particular, pantothenate, "is withdrawn from the body at an alarming rate and must be replenished," Dr. Hochberg asserts. Additionally, "during stress there is an increased withdrawal of minerals from the system." Dieting, the great American pastime, also places stress on the body. Since many people already eat foods deficient in proper nutrients, when they go on a diet and reduce their intake, the nutrients already lacking are virtually eliminated, making them more susceptible to disease.

Are Vitamins Harmful?

One of the arguments constantly given against vitamins is that they can be toxic, according to doctors Carolyn Reuben and Joan Priestley, authors of *Essential Supplements for Women:*

> There is a government agency which takes reports called in by doctors on side effects and toxicity's of drugs and vit-amins. All the toxic reactions or side effects ever reported, *total,* for all the vitamins used by millions of people in this country, for all the years that this agency has existed, are less than the toxic reactions and side effects reported *every year* for *each* of the ten drugs most commonly used in America.

Biochemist Patrick Mooney, author of *Supernutrition,* states that only one person in the past twenty-five years *may* have died from vitamin overdose. On the other hand, drugs are potentially lethal. Drug misuse and overdoses can and do kill thousands of people every day. Yet there has never been a documented fatality or report of permanent damage or injury as a result of taking vitamin and mineral supplements.

Vitamins and Minerals: How Much and When?

Taking vitamin and mineral supplements in combination is the best way to use them effectively. Your vitamin supplement program should consist of everything from vitamin A to the mineral zinc—everything in proper balance.

Fortunately, our local health food stores now have products that have all the vitamins and minerals combined, with the nutrients in proper balance, so that you don't have to read hundreds of books to figure it all out. Look at the label to see if the formula is complete, and also check the fillers if you are allergic to such things as lactose, corn, soy, wheat, or yeast. Dr. Earl Mindell's *Live Longer and Feel Better with Vitamins and Minerals* is an excellent book on vitamin supplements.

Our Drugged Society

Because doctors have been quick to prescribe antibiotics, even for viruses like colds for which they are ineffective, and because patients have prevailed upon doctors for these drugs, we now have a crisis in health care. An increasing number of antibiotics are no longer effective against certain infections, and new strains of bacteria are now appearing for which there are no available antibiotics.

I overheard a young woman who told her friend she had developed a slight bladder infection. Her friend suggested she try cranberry juice, an old remedy useful for this condition. "Oh no," she replied, "I want something that's going to work instantly, so I went to my doc and got some antibiotics." The quick fix is what we're after, regardless of the side effects. Another woman had her doctor prescribe an antibiotic for her cold, even though they both knew it was useless to cure colds. We are so programmed to reach for a drug first, prescribed or over-the-counter, that we overlook the fact that drugs are synthetic chemicals and all of them are toxic to some degree. When we take penicillin, for instance, it may kill the infection, but it also kills some of our helpful intestinal flora, and we'd be wise to take some acidophilus (found in some yogurts) to counteract this or we may be setting ourselves up for a yeast infection.

"Prescription drug-related morbidity and mortality represents a serious medical problem that urgently requires attention," says J. Lyle Bootman, Dean of Pharmacy at the University of Arizona. "Prescription-drug related problems, caused by patients not taking their drugs properly, or being prescribed the wrong drug, and side effects ranging from rashes to death, cost an estimated $75 billion in medical bills, represent 28 percent of all hospitalizations, and cause about 119,000 deaths a year." The study was presented by Bootman and Jeffrey A. Johnson at the American Medical Association science writers' meeting in 1999. With over 100,000 deaths per year, drug-related problems have now become the third leading cause of death in America, second only to heart disease and cancer, and edging out strokes as the third cause.

The U.S. General Accounting Office reported in 1998 that 102 of the 198 drugs approved by the FDA between 1978 and 1986 had serious post-approval risks, such as "heart failure, convulsions, kidney and liver failure, birth defects and blindness." We have recently seen examples of these risks with the diet drug Phen-Fen, and the diabetes drug Rezulin, now pulled from the market. Since 1997 the FDA has recalled nine drugs due to deaths. Since all drugs are dangerous to some degree, another key to staying healthy is to take as few as possible, and refrain from filling your medicine cabinet with over-the-counter medications. People sometimes forget that, although you don't need a prescription for these, they are nevertheless drugs. Certainly there are times when medications are necessary, so use common sense, but don't overdo it. Whenever it's feasible, use natural remedies.

The Magic Power of Exercise

Don't expect to be healthy all your life if you're not willing to exercise, because it's absolutely essential. Besides keeping our bodies healthy, exercise also improves our emotional well-being, keeps our mental capabilities sharp, relieves tension, and can even help overcome such serious problems as depression. Any good aerobic routine (that means *nonstop* aerobics), that speeds up the heart and breathing rates, done for a minimum of twenty minutes at a time, at least three times a week, will pay big, life-long dividends.

Exercise also relieves anxiety, counteracts anger and hostility, improves sleep and memory, and encourages a more positive self-image and greater self-confidence. People who exercise regularly feel better about themselves than people who don't. In fact, there seems to be a direct connection between physical activity and personal well-being and contentment.

The National Center for Disease Control reports that if you don't exercise regularly, you're endangering your heart almost as much as if you smoke. The CDC concluded from its studies that lack of exercise is as strong a risk factor for cardiovascular disease as smoking, high blood pressure, or high cholesterol, and further stated that a sedentary lifestyle appears to be a greater threat to the health of American hearts than these other factors.

According to the American Cancer Society's analysis of more than one million people, researchers found that the overall death rate from cancer was lowest in those who exercised regularly, during work or play, and it was highest in those who never exercised. The data also indicated that people who exercise moderately have significantly lower rates of lung, colorectal, and pancreatic cancers.

Exercise contributes to developing self-discipline. Psychiatrist Thaddeus Kostrubala, author of *The Joy of Running,* says that running works because it changes personality patterns. People develop a greater sense of their own value. They feel an increased sense of personal strength. Growing evidence also suggests that people who are aerobically fit may also have an edge intellectually. Researchers are convinced that exercise can improve concentration, creativity, and problem-solving abilities. Twenty percent of the blood flow from the heart goes to the brain. During exercise, when the heart is pumping hard, that blood flow is increased. That means there's an increase of oxygen to the brain, helping us to think. According to a study reported in *Prevention* magazine, a test on elderly people who often complain about memory lapses showed that older people put on a four-month brisk walking program improved in six out of eight mental ability tests, including reaction time and short-term memory. The sedentary control group showed no improvement.

A study on depression showed that jogging five days a week for a ten-week period was associated with significant reductions in depression scores. Among the depressed subjects who jogged, negative states of anger, hostility, fatigue, inertia, and anxious-ness decreased. Positive states of cheerfulness and energy increased. In fact, in many cases depression among older people is the result of a lifestyle of physical immobility. Inactivity is a form of self-abuse.

Aging and Exercise

There is no drug or potion in existence that holds as much promise for health in old age as regular exercise. It's the closest thing to an antiaging pill. With age, the heart's ability to trans-port oxygen and nutrients via the blood steadily declines. But your heart will stay strong and efficient if you put it to use regu-larly through exercise. Numerous studies have shown that peo-ple in their sixties and seventies can become as fit and energetic as people thirty years younger simply by participating in a pro-gram of regular walking, swimming, jogging, or other forms of aerobic exercise. Getting older doesn't have to mean getting more fatigued, but the sedentary body wears out at the slightest effort. One of the greatest benefits of exercise is the additional energy people have when they become fit. Some people complain that they're too tired to exercise but the truth is the reverse—they're tired because they *don't* exercise. Regular exercise gives you more vitality, stamina, and energy by bringing more oxygen to the brain.

In order for exercise to improve the cardiovascular system, it must be continuous, uninterrupted, and steady. Stop-and-go exer-cise, such as tennis, golf, strenuous housework, or square danc-ing, simply do not bring about metabolic, cardiovascular and muscular changes, nor do they contribute to weight loss. Only sustained, nonstop aerobic exercises put a demand on all the muscles of the body, including the heart muscle. But exercise doesn't have to be strenuous in order to be beneficial; you don't have to jog ten miles every morning before breakfast. Brisk walk-ing (three to four miles per hour) is one of the most pleasant and beneficial exercises there is. A half-hour walk at a fast pace, done at least three times a week, will give you extra energy, drive calcium into the bones to prevent osteoporosis, improve your cardiovascular system, muscle strength and flexibility, improve your mental well-being, your posture, and help you keep a trim figure.

Just as you cannot be in optimum health without proper nutrition, so too you cannot be totally healthy unless you are willing to exercise at least three times a week, preferably five, for a minimum of twenty minutes, preferably thirty. Every muscle in the body should be exercised every single day. It's because we fail to do this that we suffer so many little aches and pains. Many headaches, backaches, constipation, arthritic-type pains, and so forth, could be completely eliminated simply by getting ourselves on a program of regular exercise. It could even be a lot of fun!

Stress Reduction

In our tense world, nothing is more important than learning how to relax. When we take a little time out of each day to let go and relax, the endless onslaught of worried thoughts and images is replaced by a quiet, peaceful state that brings health to the body and mind. The multiple sources of stress in modern life create prolonged tension, and this impacts our health, happiness, and productivity. The most frequent problem the average doctor sees today is chronic fatigue, which no pill can cure, but it can be alleviated by taking the time to stop, breathe deeply, and release the tension from one's muscles, thereby allowing more energy to flow to the brain.

To the person skilled in relaxation, the payoffs are great indeed. With skill in muscle relaxation, you can improve your physical health, learn faster, conquer anxiety, work more efficiently, cope with stress, enjoy more harmonious interpersonal relationships, and discover more joy in your life. Tension is muscular tightness. Muscles in the forehead, neck, shoulders, abdomen, or other areas tighten up and stay tense when one is in a conflict situation, or in a demanding job, or rushing to get to work. Eventually those muscles begin to ache from being too tense too long, and one then discovers a tension headache, a pain in the neck, or backache. You are usually not aware of persistent muscle tension because you slowly get used to it and accept it as something to be expected. You are simply unaware that your muscles are more tense than required for the work they are doing. When you've learned to relax, however, you can also learn to become aware of mounting tension before it causes a headache or other pain such as carpel tunnel syndrome. By attending to your muscles, you can talk to them and tell them to relax and let go.

Although it may sound contradictory, the skill of relaxation actually increases energy. This is because tension inhibits muscle resiliency, and vital energy is wasted. Relaxed muscles, on the other hand, conserve energy and stand ready to move when necessary. Relaxed voluntary muscles also lead to relaxation for the rest of the body, including involuntary functions. Ductless glands stop secreting stimulants into the blood and the digestive system slows its churning. The heart eases its strained pumping against constricted blood vessels. The blood pathways, in turn, open to let life-giving blood flow easily throughout the body. A person skilled in relaxation is a vibrantly energetic person whose energy springs from a relaxed, healthy body.

Chronic tension affects learning and emotions, too. A tense person cannot learn difficult concepts or solve complex problems as well. The more tense she is, the less able she is to master the material and grasp concepts. Her emotional responses are often exaggerated and irritable. On the other hand, the skilled relaxed person can work long hours, and sleep deeply and soundly. She discovers an enlarged capacity for learning and memory, and is lively, energetic, and alert. And she usually enjoys warm interpersonal relationships.

A study with a group of forty-two hypertensive patients compared the effects of no treatment to a program of progressive muscle relaxation over a period of eight weeks. The results support the findings from other investigations that relaxation training results in decreases in resting systolic and/or diastolic blood pressure in patients with essential hypertension.**

One of the best ways to learn to relax is through practicing meditation, discussed in a previous chapter. Two good books on this subject are *The Relaxation Response* by Dr. Herbert Benson, and *A Guide to Stress Reduction* by L. John Mason, Ph.D.

A Long Healthy Life to You!

The body expresses that which we are—an instrument for the expression of the soul. It is a representation of the thoughts we have selected. An ancient adage states: "The gods we worship write their names on our faces." If you will choose predominately positive emotions, eat properly, and exercise daily, you need never be sick. Think of the money you'll save, in addition to the happiness you will experience from having a strong, healthy, energetic body all of your life!

Health is a positive state of wellness, available to you if you take charge of your own well-being. The medical crisis in this country will end when people take responsibility for their illnesses, and realize that what causes most sickness is the way they are living their lives. Dr. Blair Justice says: "By examining our attitudes toward illness, and toward our life, we may discover how we disease ourselves and, subsequently, how we may recover the ability to help ourselves in the healing process."

** Archives of *General Psychiatry,* June, 1982.

There is a mental state so happy, so glorious, that all the rest of life is worthless compared to it.

RICHARD MAURICE BUCKE, M.D.,
Cosmic Consciousness

ELEVEN
Cosmic Consciousness: The Ultimate Goal

In the earlier chapters, we discussed how Spirit has been progressively evolving through the atomic, mineral, plant, and animal phases, and finally to humankind. It appears that it still has one more phase of development before it finally merges back into itself, the All. This sixth phase is termed the Cosmic or Divine phase of creation. We know that this phase exists because we have had individuals in our history who have entered consciously into it while they lived on earth, and they left the record of their lives and deeds as a model for us to aspire to. These cosmically conscious men and women were living in a state of awareness far advanced over those of the ordinary people we deal with in our everyday existence, those who are locked into the human phase and cannot conceive of anything beyond the material world.

Cosmic consciousness means *the state of awareness or knowledge you have when you become consciously aware of the organization of the universe and of your oneness with it.* Furthermore, you will be able to translate this knowledge into a living experience.

Figure 7 below illustrates there are three forms, or levels, of consciousness: simple, self, and cosmic, and we can symbolically place everything that exists on this continuum. The first section represents the lowest forms of life with just simple consciousness—from inorganic matter to the least evolved human being, primitive man. The second portion begins with primitive man and ends with the highest type of individual, such as Albert Schweitzer, Buddha, or Socrates. The third portion represents the lowest type of cosmic consciousness on up to the fully developed divine awareness typifying the perfect human being.

Everyone is situated somewhere on this scale, and just as in the human realm, we have many degrees of human awareness, so also in the cosmic. Down through the ages there have been a number

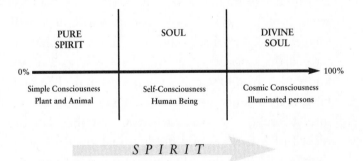

Figure 7. The Continuum of Consciousness.

of individuals who have developed this power of transcendent realization. Some of them are chronicled in an extremely interesting 1901 book, Dr. Maurice Bucke's *Cosmic Consciousness*. The individuals he discusses in this book obviously don't represent all the people who have ever had an illumination and developed cosmic awareness, but it provides an extensive history of the Illuminati before the twentieth century. In this definitive work, Dr. Bucke delineates the characteristics of the cosmic-conscious person, someone who has had an illumination. He explores the lives of people such as Spinoza, Emerson, Walt Whitman, Dante, Buddha, and Christ, who, according to his criteria, had the cosmic sense to a greater or lesser degree.

Dr. Bucke writes:

> The prime characteristic of cosmic consciousness is a consciousness of the cosmos, that is, of the life and order of the universe. With self-consciousness one is concerned mainly with oneself. With cosmic consciousness one extends his perception to the entire universe. Along with the consciousness of the cosmos there occurs an intellectual enlightenment or illumination which alone would place the individual on a new plane of existence—would make him almost a member of a new species.
> . . . The trait that distinguishes these people from others is this: their spiritual eyes have been opened and they have seen. . . . A person is identified as a member of this family by the fact that, at a certain age, he has passed through a new birth and risen to a higher spiritual plane.

Of course, this doesn't mean that when you have cosmic consciousness, you know everything about the universe. We all realize that, at about two or three years of age, when we acquired *self*-consciousness, we didn't automatically know everything about ourselves; on the contrary, after a great many thousands of years of experience, as members of the human race, we still know comparatively little about ourselves. So, neither does a person know all about the cosmos merely because one has an illumination, but that individual does have a vastly increased awareness over the merely self-conscious person. Just as there are varying degrees of human consciousness, so also in the cosmic. This fact accounts for the differences in reports on the nature of the universe by those who have achieved cosmic consciousness; such as Christ, Buddha, and Socrates. Although all contain the central truths that are nearly always identical, there are variations in their perception and reporting of these principles.

Dr. Thurman Fleet, founder of Concept-Therapy, states:

> The spiritual life is the highest expression of Spirit, exemplified by such attributes of character as love, generosity, aspiration, kindness, and so forth. . . . Very few mortals have attained to the highest form of consciousness, that of the cosmic, and usually when they do such individuals are hailed as saviors of the world. When we fully realize the meaning of these terms and the mysteries they represent, we discover that, while it may have been the special mission of one, such as Christ, or Buddha, to undertake the work of enlightening a particular age, there are many other masters or illuminated souls engaged in other work, both on this plane, and on many other planes of existence, who are interested in helping to advance the consciousness of the world.

To move into the Divine or Cosmic Phase, one must develop and learn to rely on intuition instead of the much poorer tool, reason. Intuition is the chief characteristic of the cosmic individual. It can be cultivated, but the bargain intuition drives is that it will serve you, if you serve it. We must train this latent faculty and learn to obey it in order to retain the use of it. As discussed in chapter 8, one of the primary ways to develop intuition is through meditation. We must become increasingly aware of the inner world and constantly tune our consciousness toward it. What we are seeking is *habitual, spiritual consciousness,* not "Sunday morning" spiritual consciousness that throws a dollar into the collection plate and then forgets about it for the rest of the week, but a constant awareness of our oneness with all of life.

Dr. Bucke states:

> The immediate future of our race is indescribably hopeful. The germ of cosmic consciousness has been planted in many individuals and, as this germ grows, more and more people will come into an understanding of this higher state until finally the majority of the race will have some degree of the cosmic knowledge. Then the human soul will be revolutionized. . . . Men and women will know that God is within them; that the world is ruled by immutable laws, and by knowing the laws they will know that it is beneficial to obey them. Each act performed will be an act for the Divine, each day lived will be a day dedicated to the Divine. . . . Each soul, through imparted knowledge, will

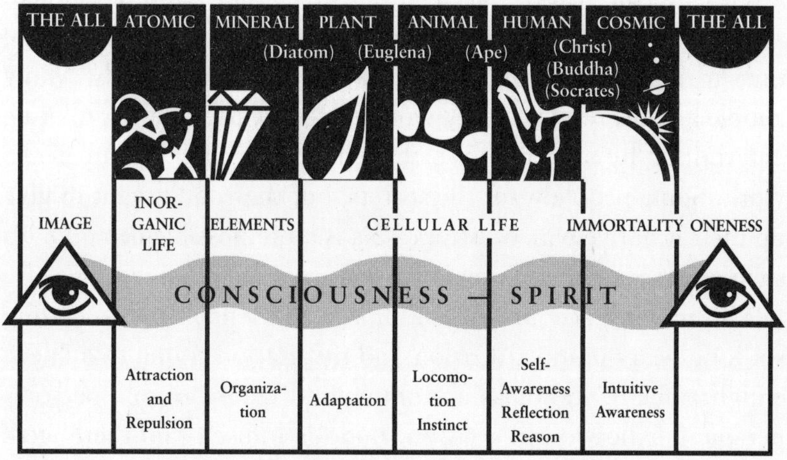

Figure 8. The Evolution of Consciousness.

know and feel itself to be immortal and will know that the
entire universe with all its good exists for, and belongs to
it, forever. Each person will come to know that violation
of spiritual laws does not pay, and each will begin to pattern his or her life according to the real, and peace and
happiness will be abundant everywhere.

Cosmic consciousness comes to the person who learns, and
lives by, the higher spiritual principles that govern life. Merely
knowing about the cosmological laws, but not living by them,
will not place you into higher consciousness; you must become
one with the cosmic by obeying the laws involved.

You may have a very great desire to attain cosmic consciousness, but if your willpower is weak, you will accomplish nothing.
The will can be trained, and it *must* be trained over and over
again until, by a natural habit, it will do the bidding of the higher
self. Dedication is one of the most important factors in this
accomplishment. When a person is a disciple of the higher path,
he or she must be resolute about the quest. The word *disciple*
comes from "discipline," meaning training of the mind or character. Until the will has been sufficiently trained and developed,
all progress is rendered utterly impossible. Yet how few take the
time to develop the will. How few develop their minds. Many
people are just too lazy; they would rather watch television, or be
entertained by someone else than put their own brain cells to
work. Some people want the secrets, but they don't want to give
up their negative way of living. This is an impossible demand. To
such a person, higher knowledge will never be obtained.

The moving account of Buddha in the wilderness, spending
six long years in mortification and meditation trying to achieve
enlightenment, stands as a monumental record of one person's
personal dedication to a vision. Buddha himself said there were
many times during that long wait when he was "almost overcome by the terrors of the dark forest," and the austerities he
had imposed upon himself. When people seek enlightenment

with such singlemindedness, they are sure to get it. Many people express a desire for cosmic consciousness, but how many are willing to exert the enormous courage of a Buddha as he faced the fears and trials of his lonely vigil?

We must also realize that Spirit is limited by the medium through which it expresses itself. For instance, it is much more limited in its expression through a little bird than through a human being. The Creative Power that fills the universe is in and of itself perfect, but its expression through our medium depends upon the condition of that medium. A good analogy is that of beautiful music being played by a large symphony orchestra in an acoustically perfect music hall, which is then recorded and transmitted by a radio broadcasting station and received by numerous stereo sets in the area. Some of these sets are in excellent condition with speakers and amplifiers having sufficient capacity and quality to express the music perfectly. In others, the receiving equipment is imperfect, and, as a consequence, the same beautiful music is expressed imperfectly. So it is with us. The Creative Power that fills our universe is perfect in itself, but its expression through our particular form depends upon the condition of our medium. Through constantly learning to contact our inner self, we can get our life in tune with the Great Conductor of the Universe, thereby becoming a perfect expression of Spirit Within. This is our task as human beings.

In one of the Concept-Therapy texts, Dr. Fleet states that:

> There seems to come a time for all of us when we become weary of pursuing outer sensations, and our attention reverts to the world within. Trying to figure out a solution to the problems of life, we become seekers after truth. Our consciousness is then led inward and, if we persist in our journey, we finally become aware of the orderly arrangement of the universe. We become cognizant of a great, all-pervading Power which rules everything and, as we progress, we try to learn more about it. No longer does

the material world absorb all our attention. Something new has come into our lives: a desire to know about the inner or spiritual world. We then enter the path leading to cosmic consciousness.

New life seems to come: our vitality is rejuvenated; we eagerly absorb all that we can. We study, we meditate, and in our studying and meditation we find, here and there, a bit of truth. These bits we hoard and treasure until we have many which we attempt to put together, like a child working with a jigsaw puzzle. At long last one great truth dawns upon us: the world and everything in it is governed and operates by laws—great cosmological principles.

Now we ask: what are those laws? We go here, there, seeking, seeking. This quest goes on and on. If we persist in our struggle for an answer, sifting through the heterogeneous maze of philosophies, religions, treatises, we will find that which we have long sought, the truth of the cosmic organization. We take a firm hold on the Eternal Principles of Natural law and, as we learn them, we become conscious of something new having entered our lives: an awareness of the One. We are now truly on the Path of Attainment, having entered a higher state of consciousness, that of the cosmic.

This, then, is our goal, the goal toward which we are all striving, whether or not we are aware of it. Spiritual men and women are the saviors of the world, and the spiritual person is also the creative one. By definition, a spiritual person is, to a high degree, united with the Divine aspect of his or her being. That individual's life and thoughts proceed from the spiritual realm, thus bringing a creative life into the world that is not dictated by the lives of others; it is an original creation. The truly spiritual person always changes the world in some way. Nearly all of the good, inspirational, and uplifting thoughts of this world have been produced by the spirit of idealists such as Plato, Kant, Schweitzer, Spinoza, and poetic souls like Walt Whitman.

Only when we are grounded in the certainty that we are a manifestation of the Divine Consciousness within our physical form do we cease to feel lost and alone. It is the experience of the Infinite that enables us to break through the isolation, anxiety, and estrangement of self-conscious existence. Spirit is all-pervasive in the universe, and we are totally dependent upon this consciousness for our existence. In the certainty of the knowledge of the omnipresent Spirit, we can achieve inner peace. God is not a patriarchal being but, for lack of a better word, an Energy Force that our limited, finite consciousness is powerless to comprehend. Yet the conscious awareness that everything and everyone *is* its existence means that we are in a holy place even when we are in the most worldly place, for everything is rooted in the Divine Life. In the words of the great theologian Paul Tillich: "If one always experienced the Divine Presence, there would be no difference between the sacred and the secular, because this difference does not exist in the Divine Consciousness."

When you fully understand the real meaning that you are a radiant expression of the Divine Spirit in manifestation, your behavior is always governed by that one central concept. Your religion is not what you claim to believe in; it is what you do with your life. What are your ultimate concerns? To what have you dedicated your life, your thoughts and actions? That is your true religion. Socrates taught that a person who really understands truth and the idea of goodness can never act against that idea. That person's entire existential relationship to life will be motivated, governed, and directed by his inner, existential relationship to the Divine; thus, it would be impossible to be unfaithful to that illuminated understanding.

Having outlined the task that lies before us, how shall we attain this goal? Naturally, it will not be an easy job, but a lifelong struggle requiring endless vigilance and rigorous self-discipline for we are indeed giving up a part of ourselves—our egotism. If we seek to know our spiritual nature, we must be prepared to sacrifice; we must be prepared to analyze our emotional make-up and systematically eliminate all of our negative, destructive traits. If we seek to walk the upper path, we must first pass through the doorway marked "Initiation." There is a probationary period we must go through before achieving enlightenment and being led into the full illumination. In every school of learning, a student must pass the necessary entrance requirements before being accepted. It is the same with the higher consciousness. This learning cannot be forced; it evolves through a person by a natural process as one evolves his or her own consciousness through studying, meditating, and living life.

Once we make the conscious decision to align ourselves with the spiritual world, persistently endeavoring to overcome our lower nature, we seem to receive help from some unseen force. That, at least, is what all the great teachers have told us; and we can feel safe in believing that help will come to us through one avenue or another. We are never alone in our battle if we are willing to turn to Spirit Within for assistance. If we persist in our determination, in our singlemindedness, insight and strength will come to us in various ways and from various sources. Here, knowledge of the path ahead is invaluable, as well as the cultivation of the love of wisdom. In a sublime sense, when we study the works of great thinkers who have crossed the threshold before us, our insight is awakened through appreciating theirs; and we may discover inner realms they long ago explored. Dr. Fleet writes: "When a person reaches a certain stage of spiritual consciousness, there comes a time when he is able to see without eyes, and to hear without ears. This individual is in touch with another world, one that is more real than this physical world. One becomes truly conscious of his Divinity and his immortality, and that is precisely the condition that all mankind yearns for, even though they may not be conscious of it."

There are many aspirants for the spiritual plane of life, but not many are able to attain it. As recorded in Scripture: "Many are called, but few are chosen." This simply means that very few people have the necessary determination to keep on with the struggle until they discover the light on the path. Usually an aspirant for the higher consciousness has been brought to it by suffering much from the superficialities of the world. She has experienced much that life has to offer and has become weary and satiated. Suffering makes her long for a higher life, and her inner cry is heard echoing throughout the universe. She is then led here and there to the knowledge that will enable her to find the higher path. Now a candidate for the more advanced spiritual expression, as she earnestly attempts to achieve self-mastery, she begins to attract assistance to herself. Through the medium of the laws of resonance and vibration, she draws to herself kindred souls, from this plane and others, who enrich her mentally and spiritually.

This type of person is attaining great wisdom. He knows intuitively that clinging to the lower self will mean that the path will be beset with difficulties and repeated pains, sorrows, and disappointments. At times, while fighting the inner battle, he secures brief glimpses of the beauty of the spiritual realm, and knows that it is the One Reality. The spiritual realm is one of inward harmony, of perfect justice, of eternal love. As time goes on, he begins to recognize the Oneness of all life and realizes that he can no longer harm others because all life is One; therefore, hurting another means harming himself. Simultaneously, this person recognizes that helping another also means helping himself, and the truth of "It is more blessed to give than to receive" becomes a reality in his life.

Dr. Fleet states:

> As you overcome your lower self, as you overcome the things which people love most and cling to with such fierce tenacity, the ego and physical pleasures, you will have left behind all confusion. You will enter into a profoundly beautiful simplicity, one which may be frowned

upon as foolish by the worldly-wise who are enmeshed in their network of error. You will have realized the highest wisdom, and you will be at peace. Having entered the region of reality, you will accomplish everything without striving, and all problems will easily be faced and handled by you. You will concern yourself not with changing events, but with the unchanging *principle* behind all things. Having yielded up your negativity, your egotism, your will to power, your biases and prejudices, you will enter into possession of the knowledge of higher worlds. As you surrender all without reservation, you will gain all; and you will find "the peace that passeth all understanding."

There are four levels of imaging: the physical, mental, emotional, and spiritual. We live on all four planes and must take care of every aspect of our being. An all-embracing affirmation I particularly like is: "I am becoming aware of my oneness with the Infinite." This fulfills the law Christ expressed as "Seek ye first the Kingdom of Heaven, and all else will be added unto you." You might try saying this affirmation as you fall asleep each night; you'll be surprised at the difference it will make in your life!

Affirmations such as this can help us achieve, in our long progress of evolution, the sixth phase of creation, cosmic consciousness. Eventually, some day, in another dimension of awareness, we shall achieve the final destiny of the evolution of consciousness, complete unity of Spirit with itself, the merging of our self-consciousness back into the One, but with greater understanding and enlightenment.

As Dr. Fleet states:

Only when we have ceased to rely on our perishable, physical self, and learned to trust in boundless measure the Creative Power, are we prepared for unity with the

One. Then for us there will be no more regret, nor disappointment, nor loneliness, nor remorse; for where all selfishness has ceased, these sufferings cannot be. When we realize the profound simplicity of spiritual consciousness, and have an unbiased, tranquil, blessed state of mind, we will know that whatever happens to us is for our own good. We will be content, and no longer the servant of the self, but the servant of the Divine. We will have nothing to defend, nothing to conceal, nothing to attack, and no interests to guard; therefore, we will be at peace.

To become one with the Infinite is the goal of man, and is a far greater possession than anything else the world has to offer. The man or woman who attains it will know the secret of immortality.

Appendix A
Relaxation Process

First, turn down the lights and make sure the room is quiet so you won't be disturbed. Loosen any tight clothing, and make yourself perfectly comfortable in every way. Now you are going to relax, thoroughly relax, from head to toe. Starting with your breathing, take three deep breaths, very slowly, and with every breath you will go deeper into a state of profound relaxation.

Now your breathing is returning to normal, but with every breath you take you are relaxing even further. You are now breathing in a calm, regulated manner, forgetting the cares of this day, thinking of nothing but your own bodily process of relaxation, and allowing yourself to drift down even deeper.

Now, starting with the head, all the muscles in that area are beginning to relax. Around the skull, the forehead, deep within the head area, complete relaxation of those muscles is now taking place, so there is no tension whatsoever in this area. Now this relaxed feeling is going into your eyes, your eyelids, and deep within your eyes, relaxing all the tiny muscles in and around and behind your eyes; letting your eyelids just feel loose and limp, and relaxed. No tension whatsoever.

The relaxation is now traveling down your face, to the muscles of your cheeks, your mouth, tongue, and on down to your jaw, relaxing all of the muscles of the chin. Just letting go of all tension and enjoying this deep, calm, relaxation. This wonderful relaxed feeling is now going into your neck, around the throat, to the back of your neck, so that your entire head area is now completely relaxed.

This relaxed feeling is now going into your shoulders, releasing their tension; just letting go, letting go completely, relaxing every muscle in this part of your body, and traveling down your arms, to your hands and fingers. Now your shoulders are feeling loose and limp and relaxed, and a warm but pleasant heaviness descends down your body as you rest here in perfect relaxation, thinking of nothing but the peace of the moment.

Now your chest area is responding to this feeling of restfulness, so that all tension in that area is completely released. Your breathing is perfectly relaxed and regular, and there is complete relaxation in your upper torso. You are now relaxing your stomach muscles—more and more—so that with every breath you take you will allow yourself to drift down even deeper.

This relaxed sensation is now traveling down your back, down that wonderfully intricate spinal cord that connects all of the nerves of your body, and branching out from it to your entire nervous system, relaxing all of your nerves. Going deeper and deeper into this wonderful state of relaxation, because it feels so good to be just letting go like this and giving all of your muscles and nerves a chance to rejuvenate.

Now all the muscles and organs in the lower part of your body are relaxing. The bladder, kidneys, and organs connected with your eliminative system are completely relaxed. You do not need to picture this, just give the order to the consciousness within; relax now. There will be no muscle too tight and none too loose; every muscle will have perfect tone.

This relaxed feeling is now descending into your lower back, the pelvic region, and going down into your legs, relaxing each muscle more and more. It feels so good to be so completely relaxed. You can feel this deep relaxation in the powerful muscles of the buttocks, traveling down your thighs, legs, knees, calves, ankles, and on down to the bottom of your feet, so that now you are completely encompassed by a wonderful, warm feeling of deep peace and relaxation.

A feeling of serenity, of peace and tranquillity, is now covering your entire body, and you are responding to it, because it feels so good to be so completely relaxed like this. You feel completely calm, completely at peace. More relaxed than you have been in a long time. All the tensions of the past week have left your body, and while you are in this relaxed state, your body is in a position to begin adjusting itself and express in a more healthy way. We know that when we are completely relaxed like this we can then begin directing the Creative Power Within to make any adjustments necessary to bring your body to a more healthy expression, and it is doing so now.

Continue to rest here for a few moments while Spirit Within brings your body to a state of perfectly normal functioning.

Appendix B
Suggestions for Self-Hypnosis

The following is a sample induction talk, which you can use as is, or adapt to your own personality style. If you wish, you can tape record this talk as an aid in learning self-hypnosis. You could record your own voice, or have someone with a soft, pleasant voice record it for you.

Now that you are completely comfortable with your eyes closed, just listen to the sound of my voice, which will help relax you even further, and follow all the suggestions given.

I want you to imagine that you are going into the lobby of a large hotel, and walking up to the elevators. Press the button marked "down." When your elevator arrives, this will be your own private elevator, perfectly safe in every way, that's going to help carry you down closer to the depths of your subconscious mind.

Now the elevator is arriving, the doors are opening, and you step inside. As you look upward above the doors, you will see a panel of buttons marked from 1 to 10, and the light is now on at the button marked 1. In a moment at my count, your elevator will begin descending, going all the way down to the tenth floor, just like going into a department store and going down to the basement. When you arrive at the tenth floor, you will get off into a room that has a big, soft, comfortable bed that you can go over to, and lie down on, and have a wonderful rest.

1. Relaxation is settling over your forehead and eyelids.

2. Relax your shoulder and neck muscles.

3. Relaxing the muscles in your arms and hands. Deeper and deeper with each breath. The more thoroughly you can relax, the deeper you will be able to go into hypnosis.

4. Now you are relaxing the muscles in your entire back, all the way down your shoulders; limp and relaxed. You are so relaxed and comfortable.

5. You are beginning to drift deeper and deeper as you relax the muscles of your abdomen and let go. Let go still more. Notice your breathing. You are now breathing slowly and deeply, and with every breath you take you allow yourself to drift even deeper into self-hypnosis.

6. Now you are relaxing your hips, thighs, and buttocks, and this wonderful relaxed feeling is traveling down your legs. Every muscle, nerve, and fiber of your body is now completely, deeply, relaxed.

7. You are drifting down more rapidly now, and going even deeper.

8. Now your legs and feet are completely relaxed, and you are in a state of deep relaxation from the top of your head to the tips of your toes.

9. Now you have released all the tension from your entire body, and these tensions will not disturb you again. More and more relaxed.

10. Now your elevator has arrived, and the doors are opening, and you step into this room and see this big, soft, comfortable bed, all made up for you. And you can just go right over there and stretch out on that bed, and go now into a very pleasant hypnotic sleep.

   Total relaxation is now over your entire body. Your mind is completely at ease. Your mind is very quiet. You are now in a very pleasant, deep hypnotic sleep. And your subconscious mind is very aware of what I am saying and wants to obey all of my instructions, because you consciously desire to do so.

   While you are in hypnosis, if any emergency should arise, you will immediately return to your normal, waking state, and be wide awake and fully alert.

11. Whenever you are ready to awaken all you need to do is count from 1 to 5 and, at the count of 5, you will return to your normal, outer consciousness, feeling completely refreshed and rejuvenated in every way.

At this point insert your positive suggestions.

If you do not succeed in achieving total relaxation, use another method to deepen the relaxation, such as imagining yourself walking through the woods, and lying down on the soft, green grass, and relaxing even further.

The following are some sample suggestions that can be used for particular concerns.

To Lose Weight

From now on you are going to eat smaller meals. When you eat your regular meals each day, each meal will consist of much less food than you have been eating in the past. Your appetite is decreasing. Your appetite is now decreasing, and you are going to want much less food than you normally eat. It will be very easy for you to do this. You find that you simply do not require as much food as you have been eating, and you will not be hungry. You will be perfectly satisfied with smaller quantities of food, and you will not feel deprived of food in any way.

From now on you are going to stick to your diet rigidly, and you will enjoy it. You are going to have all the willpower and self-discipline you need to stick to this diet and it will not be a sacrifice. You will enjoy doing it, as you watch the pounds melt away every day.

From this day forward you will eat smaller, nutritionally beneficial, nonfattening meals, and you will have absolutely no desire to eat between meals. You will be able to go longer from one mealtime to another, and you will not have the need to have any snacks. When you finish your dinner you will have absolutely no desire for second helpings or for dessert, and you will easily be able to go until the next mealtime without eating anything else.

Fattening foods no longer appeal to you. In fact, the thought of eating them is repellent to you. You will no longer desire to eat fattening foods such as ice cream, candy, cakes, and pies (or whatever your particular favorite is).

At this point begin visualizing yourself stepping on the scale and seeing your desired weight. See yourself wearing clothes you could not get into before, and see others telling you how nice you look. (Take at least three minutes to do this.)

You are not going to allow anything to prevent you from reaching your desired goal of ___ pounds. And your subconscious mind is now helping you to achieve this goal, and when you reach it, you will easily be able to maintain it. This is coming true for you now.

To Stop Smoking

Your subconscious mind is now completely and totally erasing the habit of smoking from its records. It has erased all your reasons and causes for smoking. From now on you have absolutely no reason to smoke, you do not enjoy smoking. So I want you to say to yourself mentally now: "This is the end of my smoking habit. I am now a nonsmoker." As you say this, you feel very pleased about it. You are very happy that you no longer need this crutch in your life. Your habit of smoking has been entirely and completely eliminated from your life. It is completely erased from the records of your subconscious mind, which now recognizes you as a nonsmoker. You do not need to smoke, you do not want to smoke, and you do not like to smoke. You have no desire, craving, or temptation to smoke ever again. Smoking does not exist in your life. You will always think of yourself as a nonsmoker.

(At this point visualize yourself in various scenes in which you habitually smoked in the past. See yourself in these situations as a nonsmoker, feeling calm and relaxed.)

You will never feel any nervousness or irritability or any other side effects or withdrawal symptoms as a result of stopping smoking. You will not feel any discomfort from this. Instead you will feel totally healthy and energetic. You will not replace the habit of smoking with eating or any other undesirable habit. You are now a nonsmoker. Your subconscious mind now sees and accepts you as a nonsmoker. Smoking no longer exists in your life, and you feel very pleased about this. You are very proud of yourself that you are no longer addicted to smoking.

To Gain Self-Confidence

Your subconscious mind is now erasing any memory of ever having been programmed to the idea of not having sufficient confidence. Your subconscious mind is now accepting the image of your total self-confidence. From this moment on you will have no difficulty in accomplishing whatever you wish to accomplish. You have all the confidence you need to handle your life successfully. Your confidence is increasing daily. You will have no difficulty whatsoever in being completely confident in every situation. You are seeing yourself this way now.

(At this point begin visualizing yourself in situations in which formerly you had lacked sufficient confidence. See yourself smiling, happy, and confident, totally self-assured.)

As each day passes you are gaining more confidence in yourself as a person of worth and value and you are developing a true inner strength that will be of great help to you as you go about your daily life. You now have a new confident image of yourself as a person of worth and value and all of your activities will be carried out with perfect confidence, easily and effortlessly. You are now in touch with your true inner self-confidence, and you will be able to express this outwardly.

Classes in Concept-Therapy are conducted regularly
throughout the United States and Canada by the

Concept-Therapy Institute
25550 Boerne Stage Road
San Antonio, Texas 78255
1-800-531-5628

Web site: www.concept-therapy.org
E-mail: concept-therapy@concept-therapy.org
(Please send for free brochure)

Bibliography &
Suggested Reading

Adar, Robert, ed. *Psychoneuroimmunology.* Academic Press, New York, N.Y., 1982.

Allen, James. *As a Man Thinketh.* DeVorss Pub. Co., Marina Del Ray, Calif., 1994.

Amazing Medicines the Drug Companies Don't Want You to Discover! Edited by the staff of University Medical Research Publishers, Tempe, Ariz., 1993.

Andersen, U.S. *The Magic in Your Mind.* Wilshire Book Co., North Hollywood, Calif., 1998.

Anderson, Greg. *Living Life on Purpose.* Harper, San Francisco, Calif., 1997.

Bach, Richard. *Illusions: The Adventures of a Reluctant Messiah*. Dell Publishing Co., New York, N.Y., 1984.

Balch, James and Phyllis Balch. *Prescription for Nutritional Healing*. Avery Pub. Group Inc., Garden City Park, New York, N.Y., 1990.

Benson, Herbert, with M. Z. Klipper. *The Relaxation Response*. William Morrow, New York, N.Y., 1975.

Bolton, Brett. *The Secret Power of Plants*. Berkeley Medallion Books, New York, N.Y., 1974.

Boone, J. Allen. *Kinship with All Life*. Harper & Row, New York, N.Y., 1954.

Brain/Mind Bulletin. P.O. Box 42211, Los Angeles, Calif., 90042.

Bricklin, Mark. Rodale's *Encyclopedia of Natural Home Remedies*. Rodale Press, Emmaus, Pa., 1986.

Brourman, Sherry, P. T. and Randy Rodman. *Walk Yourself Well*. Hyperion, New York, N.Y., 1998.

Bucke, Maurice, M.D. *Cosmic Consciousness*. E. P. Dutton & Co., New York, N.Y., 1901.

Capra, Fritjof. *The Tao of Physics*. Bantam Books, New York, N.Y., 1974.

Chopra, Deepak. *Ageless Body, Timeless Mind*. Crown Publishers, New York, N.Y., 1995.

———. *Seven Spiritual Laws of Success*. Amber-Allen, 1995.

Cousins, Norman. *The Healing Heart*. Norton Books, New York, N.Y., 1983.

Davich, Victor. *The Best Guide to Meditation.* Renaissance Books, Los Angeles, Calif., 1998.

Davis, Roy Eugene. *Creative Imagination.* Davis Enterprises, Garret Park, Md., 1961.

Ellis, Albert. *A Guide to Rational Living.* Wilshire Book Co., North Hollywood, Calif., 1998.

Emery, Stewart. *Actualizations.* Dolphin Books, a Division of Doubleday, New York, N.Y., 1978.

Feeling Fine Affirmations. Hay House, Carlsbad, Calif., 1990.

Fezler, William, Ph.D. *Creative Imagery—How to Visualize with All Five Senses.* Fireside Books, New York, N.Y., 1989.

Fleet, Dr. Thurman. *Rays of the Dawn.* Concept-Therapy Institute, 25550 Boerne Stage Road, San Antonio, Tex., 78255.

Fontana, David. *Learn to Meditate.* Chronicle Books, San Francisco, Calif., 1999.

Franquemont, Sharon. *You Already Know What to Do.* Jeremy Tarcher, New York, N.Y., 1999.

Fredericks, Carlton, M.D. *Psycho-Nutrition.* Grosset & Dunlap, New York, N.Y., 1976.

Gawain, Shakti. *Creative Visualization.* New World Library, Novato, Calif., 1995.

———. *Creating True Prosperity.* New World Library, Novato, Calif., 1997.

Gillies, Jerry. *Moneylove.* Warner Books, New York, N.Y., 1978.

Hanna, Thomas. *The Body of Life*. Inner Traditions, Int'l Ltd., Rochester, Vt., 1993.

Hardison, James, M.D. *Let's Touch*. (Out of Print) ASIN: 0135328047

Hartman, Cherry, et al. *Be Good To Yourself Therapy*. Warner Books, New York, N.Y., 1992.

Hay, Louise L. *101 Power Thoughts*. Hay House, Carlsbad, Calif., 1994.

Hendler, Sheldon, M.D. *The Doctors' Vitamin and Mineral Encyclopedia*. New York, N.Y., 1990.

Hilgard, Josephine, M.D. *Personality and Hypnosis*. University of Chicago Press, Chicago, Ill., 1970.

Hill, Napoleon. *Think and Grow Rich*. Wilshire Book Co., North Hollywood, Calif., 1998.

Hudson, Thomas. *The Law of Psychic Phenomena*. Hudson-Cohan Pub. Co., Monterey, Calif., 1970.

Jaynes, Julian. *The Origin of Consciousness in the Breakdown of the Bicameral Mind*. Houghton Mifflin, Boston, Mass., 1976.

Jung, Carl G. *Memories, Dreams and Reflections*. Vintage Books, New York, N.Y., 1961.

Justice, Blair. *Who Gets Sick: Thinking and Health*. Peale Press, Houston, Tex., 1987.

Kelly, Kevin. *Out of Control*. Addison-Wesley, Reading, Mass., 1994.

Keyes, Ken, Jr. *Handbook to Higher Consciousness*. Ken Keyes Center, Coos Bay, Ore., 1974.

Kostrubala, Thaddeus. *The Joy of Running*. (Out of print—check Amazon.com).

LeCron, Leslie M. *Self-Hypnosis*. Signet Books, New York, N.Y., 1964.

LeShan, Lawrence. *You Can Fight for Your Life*. Evans & Co., New York, N.Y., 1977.

Mason, John. *A Guide to Stress Reduction*. Celestial Arts, Berkeley, Calif. 1986.

McKenna, John. *Natural Alternatives to Antibiotics*. Avery Publishing Group, New York, N.Y., 1998.

Merton, Thomas. *The Seven Storey Mountain*. Harcourt, Brace & Co., New York, N.Y., 1948.

Mindell, Earl, M.D. *Live Longer and Feel Better with Vitamins and Minerals*. Keats Publishing, Chicago, Ill., 1994.

Mooney, Patrick. *Supernutrition*. Stanton Press, Calif., 1984.

Murray, Michael, and Joseph Pizzorno. *Encyclopedia of Natural Medicine*. Prima Publishing, Rocklin, Calif., 1998.

Myss, Carolyn. *Anatomy of the Spirit: Seven Stages of Power and Healing*. Random House, New York, N.Y., 1997.

Nemeth, Maria, Ph.D. *The Energy of Money: A Spiritual Guide to Financial and Personal Fulfillment*. Ballantine Books, New York, N.Y., 2000.

Ornstein, Robert. *The Evolution of Consciousness*. Prentice-Hall Press, New York, N.Y., 1991.

———. *The Healing Brain*. Simon and Schuster, New York, N.Y., 1987.

Oyle, Irving, M.D. *The Healing Mind*. Celestial Arts, Berkeley, Calif., 1974.

Padus, Emrika and the editors of *Prevention* magazine. *The Complete Guide to Your Emotions and Your Health*. Rodale Press, Emmaus, Pa., 1986.

Pearce, Joseph C. *The Crack in the Cosmic Egg*. Pocket Books, New York, N.Y., 1973.

Pearson, Durk, and Sandy Shaw. *Life Extension*. Warner Books, New York, N.Y., 1982.

Peck, Scott. *The Road Less Traveled*. Simon & Shuster, New York, N.Y., 1992.

Pelletier, Kenneth, M.D. *Mind as Healer, Mind as Slayer*. Dell Publishing Co., New York, N.Y., 1977.

Ray, Sondra. *I Deserve Love*. Celestial Arts, Berkeley, Calif., 1983.

Rector-Page, Linda, N.D., Ph.D. *Healthy Healing: An Alternative Healing Reference*. Healthy Healing Pubs., 1992 (No listed address—sold at most health food stores).

Reuben, Carolyn and Joan Priestley. *Essential Supplements for Women*. (Out of print—check Amazon.com)

Rodale, J. I., *Happy People Rarely Get Cancer.* Rodale Press, Emmaus, Pa., 1970.

Schultz, Mona Lisa. *Awakening Intuition.* Harmony Books, Nevada City, Calif., 1998.

Selye, Hans, M.D. *The Stress of Life.* McGraw Hill, New York, N.Y., 1976.

Siegal, Bernie, M.D. *Love, Medicine and Miracles.* Harper Perennial Library, New York, N.Y., 1986.

Simonton Cancer Center. Pacific Palisades, Calif., 90272. (1-800-459-3424)

Simonton, Carl, M.D., et al. *Getting Well Again.* Jeremy P. Tarcher, New York, N.Y., 1992.

Teilhard de Chardin, Pierre. *The Phenomenon of Man.* Harper Collins, New York, N.Y., 1980.

Weil, Andrew, M.D. *Eight Weeks to Optimal Health.* Fawcett Books, New York, N.Y., 1988.

————. *Health and Healing.* Houghton Mifflin, Boston, Mass., 1988.

Westcott, Malcom. *Toward a Psychology of Intuition.* Holt, Rinehart and Winston, Inc., New York, N.Y., 1968.

Whitman, Walt. *Leaves of Grass.* Holt, Rinehart and Winston, Inc., N.Y., 1949.

Wilde, Stuart. *Affirmations.* Hay House, Carlsbad, Calif., 1995.

Wolfe, Sidney, M.D. et al. *Worst Pills, Best Pills II.* Pocket Books, New York, N.Y., 1999.

Wolpe, Joseph, M.D. *Psychotherapy by Reciprocal Inhibition.* Stanford University Press, Stanford, Calif., 1958.

Zibergeld, Bernie and Arnold Lazarus. *Mind Power Through Mental Training.* Little Brown & Co., New York, N.Y., 1987.

Index

Free Magazine

Read unique articles by Llewellyn authors, recommendations by experts, and information on new releases. To receive a **free** copy of Llewellyn's consumer magazine, *New Worlds of Mind & Spirit,* simply call 1-877-NEW-WRLD or visit our website at www.llewellyn.com and click on *New Worlds*.

🌙 LLEWELLYN ORDERING INFORMATION

 Order Online:
Visit our website at www.llewellyn.com, select your books, and order them on our secure server.

 Order by Phone:
- Call toll-free within the U.S. at 1-877-NEW-WRLD (1-877-639-9753). Call toll-free within Canada at 1-866-NEW-WRLD (1-866-639-9753)
- We accept VISA, MasterCard, and American Express

 Order by Mail:
Send the full price of your order (MN residents add 6.5% sales tax) in U.S. funds, plus postage & handling to:

> **Llewellyn Worldwide**
> **2143 Wooddale Drive, Dept. 978-1-56718-339-9**
> **Woodbury, MN 55125-2989, U.S.A.**

Postage & Handling:

Standard (U.S., Mexico, & Canada). If your order is:
>$24.99 and under, add $3.00
>$25.00 and over, FREE STANDARD SHIPPING

AK, HI, PR: $15.00 for one book plus $1.00 for each additional book.

International Orders (airmail only):
>$16.00 for one book plus $3.00 for each additional book

Orders are processed within 2 business days.
Please allow for normal shipping time. Postage and handling rates subject to change.

Soul Mates

Understanding Relationships Across Time

Richard Webster

The eternal question: how do you find your soul mate—that special, magical person with whom you have spent many previous incarnations? Popular metaphysical author Richard Webster explores every aspect of the soul mate phenomenon in his newest release.

The incredible soul mate connection allows you and your partner to progress even further with your souls' growth and development with each incarnation. *Soul Mates* begins by explaining reincarnation, karma, and the soul, and prepares you to attract your soul mate to you. After reading examples of soul mates from the author's own practice, and famous soul mates from history, you will learn how to recall your past lives. In addition, you will gain valuable tips on how to strengthen your relationship so it grows stronger and better as time goes by.

- Learn why soul mate relationships don't always last forever and aren't always romantic
- Learn to do your own past-life regression
- Find out how to keep your soul mate once you find him or her

1-56718-789-7, 216 pp., 6 x 9 $13.95

To order, call 1-877-NEW-WRLD
Prices subject to change without notice

The Beginner's Guide to the Recently Deceased

A Comprehensive Travel Guide to the Only Inevitable Destination

David Staume

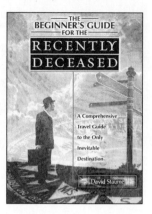

Who isn't curious to know what life is like after we die? In this humorous yet thought-provoking glimpse into other realms, David Staume asks you to open your mind and leave your body behind as he takes you on a tour of the "other side."

Find out everything you need to know about the astral realm: how to get around, what's going on, and who and what you might bump into on your travels. Explore the big questions regarding the whys and wherefores of existence: Is there a hell? What about reincarnation? Who am I? Who is God?

0-7387-0426-1, 192 pp., 5⅜ x 8, illus. $12.95

To order, call 1-877-NEW-WRLD
Prices subject to change without notice

Success Secrets: Letters to Matthew

Richard Webster

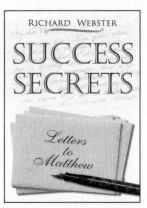

Matthew is lacking vision and passion in his life. His marriage is on the rocks and his boss is worried about Matthew's falling sales figures. Just as he is feeling the lowest he has felt in years, he goes to his mailbox and finds an envelope addressed to him, with no return address and no stamp. He instantly recognizes the handwriting as that of his old history teacher from high school. Wouldn't Mr. Nevin be dead by now? Why would Matthew get a letter from him after thirty years?

The letter and the others that follow are the backbone of this little book. Each one gives Matthew encouragement and new ways to deal with his life. After the seventh letter, Matthew sets out to find Mr. Nevin and thank him personally. Mr. Nevin's daughter in-law answers the door, and explains to Matthew that Mr. Nevin passed away five years previously. As the story ends, Matthew ponders the origin of the letters.

This little book is a quick read about following your dreams, setting goals, overcoming obstacles, pushing yourself even further, and making work fun.

1-56718-788-9, 168 pp., 5³⁄₁₆ x 8 $7.95

To order, call 1-877-NEW-WRLD
Prices subject to change without notice

Rejuvenation

Strategies for Living
Younger, Longer & Better

Joe H. Slate, Ph.D.

Preventing mutations that cause illness, keeping artery walls open and free of blockage, and prolonging the ability of cells to reproduce are reasonable expectations for anyone willing to develop his or her capacity for rejuvenation and longevity. Whatever your current age, you possess the built-in potential to repair and recreate yourself. This book offers 45 new rejuvenation strategies, many of which were developed in a college laboratory setting. By protecting and fortifying your innermost energy system, you can slow the aging process and even reverse its effects in some instances. Aging factors are flexible and responsive to deliberate intervention. When you turbocharge your inner age-defying mechanisms, you can slow the winged chariot of time and live a longer, richer life.

- Learn the Fourteen Golden Rules for Rejuvenation and eight strategies for thwarting the effects of negative stress
- Transcend biological boundaries by cultivating connections with higher cosmic energy and dimensions
- Connect with the creative power of the universe through interactions with nature
- Includes a CD with meditations and exercises from the 7-Day Plan

1-56718-633-5, 240 pp., 6 x 9   **$19.95**

To order, call 1-877-NEW-WRLD
Prices subject to change without notice

Aura Energy

for Health,
Healing & Balance

Joe H. Slate, Ph.D.

Imagine an advanced energy/information system that contains the chronicle of your life—past, present, and future. By referring to it, you could discover exciting new dimensions to your existence. You could uncover important resources for new insights, growth, and power.

You possess such a system right now. It is your personal aura. In *Aura Energy*, Dr. Joe H. Slate illustrates how each one of us has the power to see the aura, interpret it, and fine-tune it to promote mental, physical, and spiritual well-being. College students have used his techniques to raise their grade-point averages, gain admission to graduate programs, and eventually get the jobs they want. Now you can use his aura empowerment program to initiate an exciting new spiral of growth in all areas of your life.

1-56718-637-8, 288 pp., 6 x 9 $14.95

To order, call 1-877-NEW-WRLD
Prices subject to change without notice

Write Your Own Magic

The Hidden Power in Your Words

Richard Webster

Write your innermost dreams and watch them come true! This book will show you how to use the incredible power of words to create the life that you have always dreamed about. We all have desires, hopes and wishes. Sadly, many people think theirs are unrealistic or unattainable. *Write Your Own Magic* shows you how to harness these thoughts by putting them to paper.

Once a dream is captured in writing it becomes a goal, and your subconscious mind will find ways to make it happen. From getting a date for Saturday night to discovering your purpose in life, you can achieve your goals, both small and large. You will also learn how to speed up the entire process by making a ceremony out of telling the universe what it is you want. With the simple instructions in this book, you can send your energies out into the world and magnetize all that is happiness, success, and fulfillment to you.

- Send your energies out into the universe with rituals, ceremonies, and spells
- Magnetize yourself so that your desires are attracted to you, while the things you do not want are repelled
- Create suitable spells for different purposes
- Produce quick money, attract a lover, harness the powers of protection, win that job promotion

0-7387-0001-0, 5³⁄₁₆ x 8, 312 pp. $12.95

To order, call 1-877-NEW-WRLD
Prices subject to change without notice

How to Get Everything You Ever Wanted

Complete Guide to Using Your Psychic Common Sense

Adrian Calabrese, Ph.D.

When Adrian Calabrese's faithful car bit the dust, she was broke and had already maxed out seven credit cards. She went looking for her dream car anyway, and by the end of the day she was the proud owner of a shiny Jeep Cherokee. It was all because she had found the secret formula for getting what she wanted. Not long after that, money began flowing in her direction, and she paid off all her debts and her life turned around. Now she shares her powerful method of applying ancient concepts of inner wisdom to everyday life. Starting today, anyone can begin immediately to get everything out of life he or she desires.

- Follow the sure-fire six-step method for drawing whatever you want into your life
- Give yourself a psychic tune-up
- Discover your hidden talents, creativity, and artistic abilities, and use them to give your manifesting work a final blast of energy
- Use any of the sixty affirmations to help you manifest your specific goals
- Learn ways to ensure that your request to the universe has been transmitted
- Call upon the loving energies of angels and spirit guides to give extra power to your requests

1-56718-119-8, 288 pp., 7½ x 9⅛ $15.95

To order, call 1-877-NEW-WRLD
Prices subject to change without notice

Practical Guide to
Creative Visualization

Manifest Your Desires

Denning & Phillips

All things you want must have their start in your mind. The average person uses very little of the full creative power that is potentially his or hers. It's like the power locked in the atom— it's all there, but you have to learn to release it and apply it constructively. If you can see it . . . in your mind's eye . . . you will have it! It's true: you can have whatever you want, but there are "laws" to mental creation that must be followed. The power of the mind is not limited to, nor limited by, the material world. *Creative Visualization* enables humans to reach beyond, into the invisible world of astral and spiritual forces.

Some people apply this innate power without actually knowing what they are doing, and achieve great success and happiness; most people, however, use this same power, again unknowingly, incorrectly, and experience bad luck, failure, or, at best, an unfulfilled life.

This book changes that. Through an easy series of step-by-step, progressive exercises, your mind is applied to bring desire into realization! Wealth, power, success, happiness, even psychic powers . . . even what we call magickal power and spiritual attainment . . . all can be yours. You can easily develop this completely natural power, and correctly apply it, for your immediate and practical benefit.

0-87542-183-0, 264 pp., 5³⁄₁₆ x 8 $10.95

To order, call 1-877-NEW-WRLD
Prices subject to change without notice